Come Cruise with Me

in a Post-COVID World

COME *Cruise* WITH ME
IN A POST-COVID WORLD

GREG STAMM

The events and conversations in this book have been set down to the best of the author's memory.

Copyright © 2021 by Greg Stamm
Pittsburgh, PA

All rights reserved.

ISBN 978-1-7365373-2-9 (hardcover)
ISBN 978-1-7365373-3-6 (paperback)
ISBN 978-1-7365373-4-3 (eBook)

1st Edition

Book design by Anna Hall

To those who lost their lives and loved ones to COVID-19, my heart and prayers are with you.

To the first responders and other essential personnel who placed your lives on the line for others, there is no way to thank you properly.

To the staff and crew of the three-hundred-plus cruise ships that travel the seas, thank you for helping your passengers return safely home at the outbreak of the pandemic. Thank you also for enduring the loneliness and isolation of being trapped at sea for more than a year with no guests to serve. We who cruise today and in the future do so because of you.

Acknowledgements

I WISH TO thank those who turned a storyteller into a writer by suffering through a manuscript that was full of information but in need of professional help.

It began with my granddaughter, Madeline Stamm, who earned her degree in journalism and turned my sentence structure and grammar into a readable first draft.

Her other grandfather, Rich Matlak, a talented writer in his own right, was able to guide me toward presenting my stories in a more positive and less caustic manner.

Finding Kyle Fager of Your Words, LLC, to edit and refine my first draft into a piece worthy of publication was nothing short of a Godsend.

Anna Hall, our graphic designer, made the cover a work of art.

Stephen Knezovich made certain that there would be a market to which the finished product would be accessible.

I thank you, one and all.

Contents

Introduction — xi

Part 1: Better Now than Ever — 1
1. Your Post-COVID Cruise — 3
2. To Your Continued Good Health — 16
3. The Floating Hotel — 33

Part 2: The Nitty Gritty — 45
4. Sir, Would You Like Pancakes with Your Butter? — 47
5. Where to Sleep and Where to Relax — 70
6. The World's Most Customizable Vacation — 96
7. Stepping Out — 116
8. Captain, Director, Crew — 149
9. This Isn't a Private Yacht — 174

Part 3: Booking Your Best Cruise — 199
10. Now It's Your Turn — 201
11. Eeny, Meeny, Miny, Moe — 230
12. I've Made My Decision — 252

Epilogue — 260

Introduction

I WAS JUST putting the finishing touches on a book titled *Come Cruise With Me* when the coronavirus pandemic struck us all. COVID-19 not only stopped the world in its tracks; it made me realize that unless and until the cruise line industry could guarantee the health and safety of the 30 million people who cruise our oceans and seas each year, no one was going to be booking a cruise anytime soon. Neither would there be a reason to read a book about the enjoyment of cruise vacations.

As we all waited, and waited some more, for the pandemic to subside, I decided to put the book on hold until my wife and I could actually take a post-COVID cruise. This way, we could accurately report on whether this billion-dollar-a-year industry was dead in the water or if it would come back stronger, better, and healthier than ever.

Now I have answers, as we have just completed one of the very first cruises to leave the dock since ships were allowed to not only depart but also enter ports around the world. In the pages to come, I will recount our experiences and what we learned on that first post-COVID cruise, and introduce you to some of the people we met along the way.

Many characters have contributed their personalities and insights to this book, but for the purposes of this introduction, I will name just a few. I'm excited for you to get to know my new friend Nosy Nelly, whose nickname was well earned. Then there's my longtime buddy Doug, whose appetite could have made him an excellent spokesperson for any one of a hundred specialty restaurants aboard the ships sailing today. Finally, I will highlight Florence Reid, a lady of substance I have renamed Rose Dawson, owing to her remarkable similarities to the character from the blockbuster film *Titanic*.

After spending some time reading about that first post-COVID cruise, you will acquire some insight into the changes that will make your cruise vacations of the future better and safer than ever before. I will introduce you to every facet of cruising, from the myriad dining and drink options to the quality of the entertainment, to the cabins available, and to the people you will meet. You will also learn the best strategies for booking, managing the embarkation procedures, how best to enjoy shore excursions, and everything else imaginable to help make your cruise the best vacation ever.

So let's get started! I invite you to come cruise with me in a post-COVID world…

Part 1:

BETTER NOW

THAN EVER

1
Your Post-COVID Cruise

IT'S 5:00 A.M. and as usual, I'm awake and itching to get my day started. My wife remains sound asleep. If I start stumbling around our stateroom, I am certain to disturb her. So instead, I grab some writing materials and head to the ship's buffet restaurant. It seems to me there won't be too many people there at this hour. So maybe it will be just the place to find a quiet corner to sip my first coffee of the morning and write a few pages in peace.

This is a momentous day—one that has me bursting with excitement—our first full day aboard a cruise in a post-COVID world. Prior to the pandemic, my wife and I had become what you might call cruise enthusiasts. I had embarked on over fifty cruises, with my wife joining me for a large percentage of them. We had gotten into a routine where I would work for a hundred days at my law firm before taking two weeks for a cruise vacation.

Then, my batteries recharged, I would work another hundred days before we headed out on another cruise. In this way, we would take at least three cruises per year, with no sign of slowing down—right up until the crisis threw the travel industry into disarray, along with everything else in the world.

We waited well over a year to be able to do what we had come to love as our vacation of choice. We recognize that in this post-COVID world, there is likely to be a larger than usual number of people wondering just exactly what makes cruise vacations worth taking, and whether cruises will be safe in an era when we all have viral outbreaks on our minds.

As an avid cruiser with no ties to the travel industry or any particular cruise lines, it seems to me that I am uniquely positioned to provide on-the-ground insights (or on-the-ship insights, if you prefer) into why and how you should consider a cruise for your next vacation. I have not been incentivized by any cruise company, booking agent, or the travel industry in writing this book. I'm just a cruise enthusiast who thinks you should be a cruise enthusiast too, even in a world where we're living with pandemic-related stress (and in fact, *especially* in a world where we're living with pandemic-related stress). Cruises have always been the best vacations money can buy. Post-COVID, they will also be among the safest vacations money can buy.

I look forward to making the case, starting right now, on this first day of my return to cruising. There is plenty to discuss in terms of what makes cruises so great. To start, I'm excited to share what I have already learned about the changes that cruise companies have made to welcome us back in a safer and more appealing way than before the pandemic.

A New Beginning

WHEN WE LEFT our home yesterday morning, my wife and I were, as you might expect, a tad uncertain about what awaited us. After all, with the exception of essential trips to the grocery store, we hadn't done much of anything away from our home for more than sixteen months. Our flight to the port was, in a word, cathartic—and not just for us. Everyone seemed happy to be going somewhere, and we were pleased to see every passenger complying with the rules by wearing a mask and social distancing when possible.

At our destination airport, our taxi driver appeared upbeat about transporting cruise passengers once again. The security agents at the port carried similar energy as they checked our passports, our boarding documents, and our temperatures with handheld thermometers. Once we arrived at the terminal, porters wearing gloves and masks relieved us of our luggage and directed us to an entryway where we were asked a host of good questions about our health, our recent travels, and our experiences during the most active days of the virus. Finally, we were asked to produce our proof of vaccination, which I believe will be more or less mandatory on most cruise lines going forward. On more than fifty cruises prior to this one, I had always found health screenings to be rather superficial, but now they are more than adequately thorough.

We made our way to the check-in counter, where an attendant greeted us with a smile and a questionnaire to fill out while she prepared our cruise identification cards, which double as room keys. Next, she took our photos, entered them into the system alongside our information, and advised us of certain changes that had been made to the ship and the busiest venues like the dining room, the buffet, and the theater—all in the name of social distancing. We also received a booklet highlighting the measures being taken day and night to sanitize our stateroom and all public areas aboard.

Upon boarding, I couldn't help but marvel at the overall appearance of the ship. If we hadn't sailed on this ship previously, we would have thought it was a brand-new vessel. I imagine that our ship wasn't alone in creating this impression. The almost three-hundred other ships sidelined by COVID have surely been refitted and refurbished to look as new as ours.

At the buffet that first morning, I found a table in a far

corner, a spot that afforded a view out the window. Soon the sun would rise over the blue horizon, bringing life to the world and hopefully inspiration to my pen. But then, just as I began contemplating which pandemic-related changes I would write about that morning, I heard loud voices heading in my direction.

There had to have been more than a thousand seats still unoccupied at this early hour. Yet the three ladies who'd just entered chose to sit at the table directly next to mine. My concern about their proximity didn't stem from infectious diseases, as the cruise line had properly spaced every table on the ship. Rather, it was the noise level that had me internally grousing about the all-too-narrow distance between us. I would just have to tune them out and focus on my work.

"So how are you enjoying the cruise so far?" came the voice.

I had only just set pen to paper when I realized it was addressing me. "I'm impressed with the improvements," I said, a smile on my still-unshaven face. "Mostly I'm just happy to be back at sea."

"So this isn't your first cruise," the owner of the voice said. She was a pleasant-looking woman perhaps in her early fifties, her hair cropped short and carefully styled, her two friends meeting similar descriptions. "Neither is it for us. My name is Nell, by the way. These are my friends, Nancy and Marie. What's your name?"

"My name is Greg," I said as pleasantly as I could manage. I could already feel my writing time slipping away. "It's nice to meet you."

"My friends and I have been waiting and waiting for this day to finally arrive. How did you weather the virus?"

"My family and I were very lucky not to have been exposed, but our hearts go out to those who weren't so fortunate."

Nell agreed with this assessment, then launched into an explanation about how she and her friends had been sorority sisters while attending Michigan State University. Now they were spread across the country with Nancy on the east coast, Marie on the west coast, and Nell hailing from the heartland.

"We cruise once a year together," Nell explained. "So we're experienced."

Her friends tittered.

"From the looks of things," Nell continued, "the delay in starting this cruise may have been worth the wait. Last night, we ate dinner in the buffet and we never had to touch anything until we were seated at our table. Seems they got the message about the need for cleanliness and social distancing. It was a little hard to converse in the theater with every other seat taped off like that. But the show was still terrific. And it was kind of nice to have the extra space. Did you have a chance to see it?"

All I could think to ask myself was whether Nell had taken a single breath between sentences. I would have to set aside all thoughts about getting any writing done. In a sense, this came as a relief, because the book I had started writing long before COVID-19 entered our lives was one exclusively about the pleasures of cruise vacations and the people who tend to take them. Now that everything had changed, I still wasn't entirely sure how my book would have to change with it.

I must have waited too long to answer, because Nell started again.

"Today is a sea day, which we usually use to explore every inch of the ship. We're excited about it, because I've never seen a ship that looks and smells so new. Kind of like when you first sit in a new car at the dealership. Don't you agree?"

Nell did not give me time to agree.

"What's the pen and paper for? Are you writing a letter or just catching up on some work?"

"Actually, I'm writing a book. But it can wait. I'm enjoying our conversation."

"Ladies!" Nell exclaimed. "He's writing a book! How interesting. Are you a published author? What are you writing about? And what is your last name, so I can check out your other work?"

So much energy, I thought. *She surely didn't spend last night partying the night away.* She and her friends had clearly been up for at least an hour already, as well, as they were uncommonly well coiffed and attired.

"I write under an assumed name," I said, deciding to have a little fun with my unexpected company. "The subject matter is a bit off color from time to time." Surely this would keep them talking. With a bit of luck, maybe Nell would wind up providing all the information I needed to complete my new introduction to cruising.

No luck necessary. Looking back, I should have brought a tape recorder instead of pen and paper.

"Off color? Are you writing a pornographic novel?" She didn't wait for me to reply. "More importantly, do you envision passengers like us as subjects for your book?"

I laughed. "You're definitely going to be in the book, Nell, but I hate to disappoint you, as it is in no way pornographic."

They slumped, disappointed.

"Not to change the subject, but why don't you ladies tell me about your plans for the rest of the cruise?"

"A lot will depend on what we learn at the big lecture they're offering this morning," Nell said. "You can catch it in the theater or watch it on the television in your cabin. Seems as though they're going to put the cabins to better use than before COVID. Did you look at the room service menu? You can now order food from the various dining rooms and eat in your own cabin or balcony just about any time of day."

It seemed to me that Nell was already well informed on subjects that everyone aboard must have been interested to know, so perhaps I had stumbled upon exactly the expert I needed to get the book restarted.

"What can we expect from the lecture, do you think?"

"Where do you want me to start? The excursions are going to look a lot different. They tell me those overcrowded buses we always used to have to ride are only going to be half as full. There will be more excursions for smaller groups, and the times will be staggered. Instead of everyone leaving the ship at the same time lined up shoulder-to-shoulder, we'll leave at a distance in a more orderly fashion."

One of my original plans for this book was to advocate for ways to improve upon shore excursions, so this delighted me.

"I'm thinking the day trips to those private islands the cruise companies own will be better too. I wish we had a private island scheduled on this cruise. We'll have a longer time to enjoy those islands than we've had on past cruises. I've heard rumors that some cruise lines are considering overnight stays on their islands to give the ship a chance to breathe and be sanitized. Just imagine! You can enjoy a luau under the stars on the beach, wake up in your bungalow in the morning, and take a walk along the shoreline as the sun comes up. I hope the rumors are true, because that's where I want to cruise next!"

Not everyone might agree with Nell on this point, but the ships of every cruise line will definitely still be available for those who wish to eat in a less-crowded dining room, enjoy a show in a less-than-capacity theater, and sleep in that freshly cleaned and sanitized stateroom every night.

"The lecture will also cover the additional specialty dining restaurants that have been created and the expansion of the anytime-dining availability," Nell continued. "I think cruising from here on out is going to be a lot more fun and safer than in the past."

Shortly before boarding this cruise, I had created a checklist of things I wanted to see changed as we reentered the world of cruise vacations. Now, without even having to ask, Nell had filled in most of the details that allowed me to check off nearly every item.

"So if your book isn't about sex, then what is it you're writing about?"

"I'm writing a book about cruise vacations, the people who cruise alongside you and me, and the changes that had to be made before we could safely return to sea."

Nell furrowed her brow playfully. "Why didn't you tell me this earlier? I might have been able to shed some light on the subject. If you'd like, I'd be happy to share some of my experiences with you."

"That's very kind of you. For now, though, I'm still playing catchup on everything you've already told me. I should probably get writing."

"Well then how about I check in with you as the cruise progresses?"

I drew a breath to reply, but Nell had already moved on to the next idea.

"Maybe we could have breakfast together every once in a while! We're both early risers, after all."

Inwardly, I sighed at the notion that this book had suddenly become a collaborative effort. Still, I had hoped for input from my fellow passengers. I couldn't have asked for a more eager participant.

"That sounds like a great idea, Nell. I'll look forward to hearing what you've learned along the way. Don't forget, I'm also writing about people. If you happen to find someone worth engaging in conversation, I would be interested to hear about them as well."

"Ladies! We just got an assignment to keep us busy."

With that, 6:00 a.m. had arrived and the buffet officially opened for service. Nell and her friends excused themselves to fetch their breakfast, while I got down to writing feverishly. I'd come to this supposedly quiet place with good intentions, but now it seemed that I should follow one of Nell's key insights and have breakfast delivered to my stateroom.

No Place Like Home

BACK IN MY room, I found my wife wide awake and sitting beside a sumptuous breakfast. She must have been doing some mind-reading of her own.

"I ordered from the dining-room menu instead of filling out the card they left on our bed last night. Did you know that under the new policies, the room service menu is hugely expanded? We can order all the usual stuff, but they'll also deliver us anything they're serving in the dining room."

"That's great news," I said. "And this breakfast looks amazing."

After taking my seat across from my wife and diving into the eggs Benedict and juice she had ordered for me, I told her about my conversation with Nell and her friends. She thought it sounded like a great idea to enlist their help in gathering information for the book.

"So does this mean you won't have to do any research on this trip after all?" There was a hint of hope in her voice.

"No, I'll still need to do some sleuthing so we can report back on the changes we see."

"What's the research plan for today then?"

"After breakfast, I'm going to seek out the staff captain and ask some questions about security changes that have been made because of the virus."

She agreed that this sounded like a good idea.

"What will you be doing with your morning?"

"There's a lecture in the theater that's going to address changes to the way we enjoy excursions," she said. "It's supposed to outline the differing dining options and the ways we can socially distance in the theater and other venues."

"Yeah, Nelly mentioned something about that." Given the buzz about this event, suddenly it sounded like maybe I'd come up with the wrong plan. Surely the lecture would deliver a trove of key information.

"Don't worry," my wife said with a knowing smile. "I'll take notes so you can still go see the staff captain."

"I'll fill you in over lunch."

2
To Your Continued Good Health

As it turned out, the staff captain wasn't available that morning. Fortunately, one of her fellow officers was happy to give me some time to answer my many questions. Assistant Staff Captain Tom Elliott was not only gracious but also full of information about the subjects to which I sought answers.

"I'll tell you," he said as we sat down, "we're all just glad to be back to business. The hiatus was horrible for all of us who work aboard this ship. We've been roaming about for more than a year with no passengers to serve."

He explained how his crew had been heroic in the early days of the pandemic, helping passengers manage their needs until they could safely return home. Next came the long period of isolation for everyone. There was much to accomplish before the cruise line would allow the ship to welcome back passengers. Though the work kept them busy, the indeterminate time frame had made the weeks and months feel especially long.

"It was a trying time for everyone," he said.

"Can you give some examples of the changes you made?"

"Our department is responsible for the security of the vessel, the passengers, and the crew. After the crisis hit, once we were finally able to dock, the ship underwent a total overhaul from top to bottom. It's almost like being aboard a brand-new ship."

"Everything definitely does look new."

"Some of it's refurbished, but quite a bit actually *is* new. All of the furnishings were removed, including the bedding in your cabin. Next came a cleaning of the vessel like nothing I've witnessed in close to twenty years working for this cruise company. They also installed a new air-filtration system. It's similar to what's been happening in major medical centers throughout the world."

"What kinds of reconfigurations resulted from the new safety standards?"

"When we began to reconfigure the ship, we attempted to provide as much distance as possible between passengers in the public venues. This allows us to follow social distancing rules to the letter."

"What has changed about the cleaning practices?"

"I'm sure you noticed that there are more hand-sanitizing stations than ever before. And just wait until you see how the cabin stewards clean and sanitize your room each morning and evening before you go to bed. They've redoubled the cleaning practices. They'll even use an electrostatic disinfectant machine to spray down and sanitize all surfaces."

"I look forward to seeing that in action. What about from a policy perspective? What's changed there?"

"Our department has picked up a new responsibility. The word 'health' has been added to the words 'safety' and 'security.' You've seen some of this already. What did you think of the check-in and boarding process? The questions you were asked and the requirements you had to complete before you came aboard were pretty rigorous, no?"

"It was extremely impressive," I told him, "particularly compared to what I experienced on my pre-pandemic cruises."

"How many doctors and nurses did you encounter?"

I hadn't been keeping track, as I was more interested in getting on the ship and relaxing after my busy day of travel.

"Well, I can tell you that a year ago, we had one doctor, a nurse practitioner, and two nurses manning the infirmary. Today, we employ three physicians. One is an infectious disease doctor. Another is a family practitioner. The third is an epidemiologist."

"You mean we have a doctor like Dr. Fauci on board?"

"We do indeed. Along with two nurse practitioners and five nurses. We've checked the ship's manifest and know that we have at least another dozen physicians traveling as guests. We also have enough medicine to meet every known possibility."

Since the pandemic had been a worldwide event and cruise ships visit ports all over the world, I wanted to know how visits to ports of call would be handled.

"That's a very good question." He explained that unlike in past years, the contingent of security personnel who would come aboard to clear our ship and allow passengers to go ashore would include representatives from the Ministry of Health of our host port. "We've been pleased that host countries and even smaller islands are as concerned about protecting their citizens as we are about protecting you and our crew. You can expect to be asked a series of health-related questions as you exit the ship and you will be handed a list of protocols to follow as you leave the vessel. If you're taking a tour, it will be accompanied by a representative of our host port to ensure social distancing and compliance with other rules that have been put in place.

"Oh, and don't forget to bring a mask or two along with you. We've been impressed with how well this has worked so far."

"This question may sound stupid, but who's going to enforce the rules when we're aboard the ship?"

"Obviously, everyone wearing an officer's uniform is going to remind passengers, crew, and other staff when they're straying from protocols. Since officers are busy doing their jobs most of the day and evening, we also employ a security team that patrols our ship for your protection—not only for health-related issues, but for everything else that could possibly pose a danger."

"I've never seen these security teams. Is this something new?"

"It's not new, although we've expanded the team because of recent events. You wouldn't know them even if you saw them. They dress like you dress, wearing beach attire by day and whatever dress is called for in the evening."

"How interesting. Why don't they wear uniforms?"

"Well, let me ask you this. Is a shoplifter in a department store likely to commit a crime when being watched by a person in uniform? Of course not. Our security personnel are here to protect you and not follow you around. They blend into the woodwork. We're fortunate to employ them."

After thanking Assistant Staff Captain Elliott for his time and valuable insight, I left his office feeling proud of the sheer amount of information I had managed to gather on the first morning of the cruise. I had met Nell and put her on assignment, had feasted on a delicious breakfast in our cabin, and had gathered a wealth of information from a man who knew what he was talking about. My wife was certain to have a great deal more information to share from the lecture she attended as well.

Around the corner, the wall clock alerted that lunchtime had arrived already. I try not to wear a watch on vacation, as time seems so much less relevant when at sea than it does at home. Perhaps this would be as good a time as any to relax on our balcony and enjoy a burger and beer while keeping an eye out for dolphins or whales, but I still had things to write about pertaining to safety, security, and good health at sea.

After a few hours in the sun, I came inside and sat down at the desk in our suite to pick up where I had left off.

A New Normal

IF YOU COUNT yourself among the people questioning whether it is safe to cruise in the post-COVID world, consider the notion that this isn't the first time that the major cruise companies have answered questions about safety and security with sweeping, highly effective changes to the service they offer.

After September 11, 2001, the words "safety" and "security" took on a new meaning for all of us as we realized there was no place on Earth immune to terrorist attack. As we begin to leave our homes after months and months of isolation and quarantine from the coronavirus, we must again reconsider those two important words, while also including the word "health," as we discuss our travel options and concerns.

If you're old enough to remember the routinely practiced safety drill from grammar school and high school, when you were told to slide under your wooden desk and place your head between your knees in an effort to protect yourself from a nuclear attack, then you are certainly old enough to have been on a cruise or two in your lifetime. Safety in those days meant locking your doors at night, knowing where the emergency exit in a theater was located, and never walking home alone after dark. My, how times have changed.

As we return to *a* new normal (not *the* new normal, as I am certain that sometime in the future there will be a need to further define those words), we must once again ready ourselves for protection from outside forces, be they of natural origin or rendered by human hands. The question at hand: what reassures me that cruising the seas and oceans of our world in this particular new normal will be as safe as a visit to the grocery store, a sporting event, your place of worship, or your favorite restaurant?

There is an old saying that goes, "Fool me once, shame on you. Fool me twice, shame on me." Cruise companies have suffered a serious setback, if not an outright catastrophe, because of what transpired on cruise ships during the onset of the pandemic. Given the higher-profile stories about people getting sick from the virus en masse, it wasn't a good look. To me, the evidence that they have taken these matters seriously was already at hand, even before my long-awaited trip on a post-COVID cruise. The fact that I had three cruise vacations cancelled because of safety concerns in the year following the outbreak was, for me at least, plenty to convince me that my next cruise would be far safer than my last.

And it absolutely has been.

Like most people, I mostly stopped worrying about a nuclear attack after the 1980s came and went. The bombing of the Oklahoma City government building in 1995 didn't prevent most Americans from renewing their driver's licenses at their local DMV. My guess is that you eventually resumed flying on commercial jets in the years following the unforeseen attack on the World Trade Center in 2001. Did you stop going to movie theaters after the 2012 mass shooting in Aurora, Colorado? Did you swear off nightclubs after an unstable individual killed forty-nine people in Orlando one terrible night in 2018? On a more direct and personal front, did the last maniac who passed you on the thruway at one hundred miles per hour convince you that driving is unsafe?

Granted, pandemics, terrorists, and crazy drivers are different foes—different brands of disruption to daily life—but the root reaction is essentially the same (or at least it should be). Life is meant to be lived. You can't allow fear to so completely reshape your perspective that you forget to live in the first place. The initial fear that the pandemic has foisted upon us has gradually begun to lift. Now it's time to consider a few facts. First, cruise vacations have always been among the safest you can take, both from a security perspective and a health perspective. Second, life will be even safer on a cruise ship now than it ever has been.

Don't forget—there were over three hundred ships at sea when the pandemic first broke, yet only a small percentage of that number made the headlines throughout the world in the days that followed. Even with that small percentage proving the efficacy of pre-COVID sanitization measures that most cruise companies espoused, it is quite clear that the efforts have redoubled to keep these ships clean and the passengers healthy. There is a good reason for this. Cruise ships are not unused to having to make these kinds of changes.

Prior to 9/11, ships presented with much more lax physical security. It used to be that if you were a family member of someone about to embark on a cruise, you could board the ship on the day of the launch, taking in the luxury and enjoying the tangible charge of excitement that always accompanies the first day. In the 1980s, for instance, I would escort my mother to the port, park my car, accompany her aboard, help her check into her cabin, and tour the entire ship. Then, approximately one hour before sailing, I would be asked to disembark along with all the other non-ticketed visitors.

Back then, passengers from one ship could even board other ships that arrived in a port on the same day. Cruise companies used to think of these opportunities as free advertising. There was no better way to convince people of the luxury they offered than to give them free opportunities to see it firsthand.

Obviously, 9/11 changed all of that. Since that ill-fated date in September 2001, no person has been admitted access to an airport terminal, government building, sports arena, or any of a host of other facilities without first passing through a cordon of metal detectors and/or an X-ray scanner of their bodies and the luggage or handbags they are carrying on their person. Cruise ship ports and vessels are no different. The companies have dramatically changed their policies on who is allowed to board a ship, what they can and can't bring aboard, and what conduct will be allowed on-board or when the ship is docked at a port of call.

Since 9/11, whenever you arrived at the port entrance, your vehicle would be stopped and you would be asked to show your passport or other identification and boarding documents. Even your taxi driver would be required to produce identification and proper credentials. These measures were put in place to ensure that you would always be able to feel comfortable in the knowledge that you were now entering a *safe zone*, one quite a bit safer than the sometimes white-knuckling experience of riding in a taxi from the airport.

After you exited your vehicle, a host of baggage handlers would relieve you of your luggage, which you would not be reacquainted with for several hours, as it, too, would be passed through a rigorous screening of its own. If contraband or other prohibited items were discovered inside your luggage, you would be invited by the ship's security detail to explain the contents before your luggage was delivered to your cabin. Part of the reason for this was that fear of amateur bomb-making post-9/11 compelled cruise lines to initiate rules preventing passengers from bringing liquids, including alcoholic beverages, onto the ship. No wonder the ship's liquor locker always fills up so quickly.

None of these security measures have changed in this post-COVID world. Rather, they have been reinforced by a number of new efforts related to travel histories and health. When you reach the check-in counter, your passport will be copied and your picture will be taken and entered into the computer to ensure that it matches the person identified on your cruise card. This card will be your most utilized piece of plastic for the duration of your trip, as you will use it to charge purchases to your account and as your ticket to exit and board the ship at every port of call. In a post-COVID world, I anticipate more of these cards to be converted to wristband-style scanning devices, as this will help cut down on contact points.

After check-in is completed, you will be allowed to enter your ship by proceeding to the gangway, where you will scan your cruise card/wristband, empty your pockets, and proceed through an X-ray machine similar to the machines we pass through at airports. As a point of interest to those who have a pacemaker or other medical device inserted permanently in your body, you will be allowed to bypass the machine and be individually screened by a member of the security detail. I have pointed out a few minor intrusions that you will encounter in the name of ensuring a healthy voyage, but make no mistake, these minor intrusions are just that—minor. Once you are on the ship, you won't be required to wear a mask at any time. On this first post-COVID cruise, the crew wore face masks, but I think it was more about reassuring the passengers than it was about medical necessity. By the time you are reading this book, most of the intrusions mentioned will be a thing of the past, except hopefully for the changes to the buffet, where passengers won't be touching food that might wind up on your plate instead of theirs.

Welcome aboard! From here, your cruise is likely to proceed in a fashion similar to the way they have always gone, except it is a virtual certainty that your ship will be so clean and sanitized as to appear brand new. Enjoy that new car smell as you have a bite to eat, enjoy a beverage, and/or take a self-guided tour of the magnificent vessel you will be calling home for however long your cruise will last.

Don't forget that before the ship sets sail, you will be required to attend a safety drill. In the past, this drill has taken place at your assigned muster station, but most companies will modify this procedure due to social distancing requirements and instead ask you to watch a video on the television in your cabin. The message will be the same as it always had been during these safety drills in the muster station. The venue simply will have changed. Expect a few informational supplements related to health and sanitization to accompany the video as well. Later, you will be invited to locate the actual muster station in staggered intervals to ensure that people are not crowded around each other in the way they used to be for these drills. The whole affair will only take about twenty minutes of your time and it will leave everyone that much more prepared for the extremely unlikely event of an emergency at sea.

On the evening of the first day on the ship, even as you and I are topside or on our private balconies for the sail-away celebration, our captain and crew will remain hard at work ensuring a safe and sanitized voyage. As the voyage embarks, among us (although mostly out of sight and difficult to identify) will be the security team. Their mission will be to protect us from each other, sometimes from ourselves, and certainly from every outside force. Throughout the cruise, there will be crew drills which simulate the response that would be necessary if there was a fire in the kitchen, a medical emergency, or even a man-overboard event. You will never feel watched as you enjoy your vacation, but you will sleep better at night knowing that security is there if needed.

When we enter our first port of call, the ship will dock and the crew will begin the process of readying the vessel for disembarkation. If you are an early riser, you may enjoy watching as the crew casts the lines to dock attendants who secure the ship. Next comes the building of the gangway from ship to shore and the arrival of a contingent of security and other personnel from our host port. This process is called "clearing the ship" for entry to the port.

Depending on where we are in the world, the clearing process may be routine or it may be far more formal. Entering United States ports will differ considerably from entering ports in Russia, China, and the Middle East. It used to be that lines would form on the gangway during the clearing process, but COVID restrictions are likely to lead to assigned and staggered departure times for every passenger.

Either way, just as our ship's personnel were careful while allowing us to board, so too will be the security detail of our host port. Some countries require a visa, although the overwhelming majority do not. If you wish to visit Russia, for instance—which I highly recommend—be prepared to play by Russian rules and not your own.

In this new normal, expect the rules to be essentially the same on the pandemic front. Prior to the recent pandemic, port security throughout the world was more concerned about who you were and why you were visiting rather than how you felt, whether you had been vaccinated, or what countries you had been to in recent months. Personally, I welcome the idea of entering a port that is concerned about my health.

Whenever we disembark at a port of call, my wife and I bring as little cash as possible, a credit card that is universally accepted, our cruise cards, our driver's licenses, and copies of our passports. Before leaving your home, you should make a few copies of your passport to bring with you on the cruise in case you misplace one. Another safety tip is to always make sure you pre-program your cell phone with all telephone numbers that will connect you to your ship. Things can sometimes happen on shore which cause you to be late in returning to the ship. Given that it is our responsibility to be aboard on time, having the numbers to call could help prevent you from being left behind and having to find your own means of reuniting with the ship.

In this way, safety at sea is not just the responsibility of the cruise line. It is our responsibility as well. It is important to relax on your vacation, but it is also important to keep your brain alert and not leave your common sense at home. The day before we arrive in every port, the cruise director will offer a briefing on what to expect once we dock. In addition to advising us of the fun things we may do, the briefing will include safety tips on places to avoid and how we should conduct ourselves in a country that is not our own. Every country will have its own COVID protocols, but some of the other pieces of information you receive will be decidedly more eye-opening. Believe it or not, jaywalking is ticketed in several countries. Chewing gum or smoking on a public street may be fineable offenses in certain places as well.

It used to be that, in certain ports, we would enjoy numerous opportunities to stroll through town, do a little shopping, and have lunch at a local pub. Some such ports might be more restrictive about where you can and can't go in this new normal. Only you know your tolerance for this type of activity, but please promise me that you will avoid finding yourself in tight, unlit alleyways, especially after dark. Your loved ones, your fellow passengers, and the ship's officers and crew want everyone to return safe and sound.

Don't be surprised if you receive a temperature check and a sanitized wet towel to wash your hands and face as you re-enter the ship.

Over the years, friends and workmates have asked me many questions about security and safety while on a ship at sea. More recently, the main question had more to do with why I had planned a cruise so soon after the pandemic began to subside. The answer is as simple as the reason I gave for flying on an airplane within weeks of September 11, 2001. What could be safer than air travel with all of the controls that were put in place to prevent a recurrence? Does anyone actually believe that a cruise company that cancelled my last three cruises is going to re-engage customers without figuring out a safe way to do it?

In the end, what gave me peace about the safety and security of this cruise was the many measures that have been in place for the past twenty years. I also take comfort in the knowledge that despite the devastation COVID-19 has caused, it has served as a wakeup call for all of us, especially cruise line operators who will do anything and everything to ensure our safety at sea.

3
The Floating Hotel

By now, it should be apparent to all that my wife and I wasted little time in booking and now participating in our first post-COVID cruise. Truth be told, we wasted no time at all. The cruise we had hoped to take in November 2020 was also cancelled, as was the one we had then booked for January 2021. As we sat at home watching first the election of a new U.S. president and then his inauguration, we wondered if the changing of the guard would signal a change in the way we would be able to live our lives. If we were suffering from cabin fever after a year of isolation from family, friends, and the things we most enjoyed, so too must have been the rest of the world.

My guess is that whether you are a cruise enthusiast or you have never even considered this type of vacation, you and the ones you love have been itching to get away from home and take some form of vacation as soon as you can.

Many of the people I have spoken to have been consulting travel agents or perusing the Internet for places that might be both fun and safe to visit now that the travel bans have been lifted.

When you're getting close to making a decision, I ask you to include in that process the fact that a cruise ship is also something of a floating hotel, one that will lead you to many different places without the effort and stress (or for that matter, the pandemic-related risk) of packing and unpacking at every stop along the way.

Just prior to leaving for this cruise, I watched as my son packed for his first post-COVID vacation. He and his family would be piling into the SUV for a cross-country sightseeing vacation to the Grand Canyon, Phoenix, Las Vegas, and Southern California. This was, I suppose, their way of putting the cabin fever behind them, the logic being that they hadn't seen much of anything for the past year-plus, so they might as well see everything at once now that they were allowed.

Counting the number of days it would take to drive there and back, my son and his family would be on the road for sixteen to seventeen days and nights. Many, many years ago, when I was a lot younger than I am today, I took my family on a similar trip. The memories have lasted a lifetime, but I also recall the sensation of needing a vacation to rest from our vacation as soon as we returned home.

A few years ago, my wife and I flew to Milan, rented a car, and drove first to Venice, then to Florence, and eventually to Rome before flying home. The trip lasted a total of twelve days, and we slept in no fewer than six different hotels. We visited many wonderful cities and enjoyed the sites these cities offered. But by the end of the trip, we were both totally exhausted.

Packing and unpacking suitcases, loading and unloading the car, and then driving a hundred or more miles to repeat the process takes a lot of energy and precious vacation time. While this may be avoided by signing up for a land vacation with a tour company, you will nonetheless find yourself continuously packing and unpacking before boarding a bus, train, or airplane to take you to your next destination. Moreover, you will be dependent on your fellow passengers to be on time, move about at your pace, and enjoy the same things you wish to enjoy.

If you want to see many places in a relatively limited period of time, in an abundantly safe, healthy environment—all without having to pack and unpack at every stop along the way—a cruise vacation is for you.

The Journey Is the Destination

AFTER MORE THAN a year of travel restrictions, would you enjoy a vacation that includes visits to places such as Copenhagen, Denmark; Oslo, Norway; Stockholm,

Sweden; Helsinki, Finland; St. Petersburg, Russia; Gdansk, Poland; and Berlin, Germany? What if I said that you could go to all these places without having to keep unpacking and repacking your luggage at every stop? Would it make your journey less stressful knowing that someone else is leading the way and allowing you to return to your ship for your evening meal and a good night's sleep in the same bed each night of the trip? Would you like to do all of this on the same vessel, one that is thoroughly cleaned and sanitized on the regular, rather than taking a chance with a new set of cleaning procedures and distancing practices at each new hotel where you plan to stay each night?

You might consider a trip through South America that begins in Lima, Peru before cruising to Santiago, Chile. This cruise could then take you to the coast of Antarctica, the Falkland Islands, and off to Buenos Aires, Argentina. It might end in Rio De Janeiro, Brazil. Sure, you could take a flight between each of these places, but how much easier, more fun, and more luxurious would it be to travel aboard a beautiful ship with English-speaking tour guides to show you around the port cities?

Even if your vacation is only intended to appreciate the change in color of the fall landscape in the northeastern United States and Canada, wouldn't it be more relaxing to sail from New York, through Boston, and then on to Nova Scotia before entering the St. Lawrence Seaway with stops in Quebec and Montreal?

A cruise ship is a floating hotel and much more. Once aboard, you will only have to make the little decisions and let the cruise company do the hard work of moving you from place to place. Instead of spending hours in a car, at an airport, or on a train, you can relax by the pool, sipping a drink and thinking about what you will do when the ship next enters a port of call. You may enjoy a leisurely breakfast in your room or a stone's throw away in the dining room and then return to your room to dress in clothes appropriate for the day's activities.

When you're tired of shopping or sightseeing at a stop along the way, you can return to your ship knowing you are safe to enjoy a cocktail and a meal guaranteed to satisfy your tastes. Before retiring for the night on a comfortable mattress in a recently cleaned room, you may take in a show in the theater or simply sit on your balcony and count the stars.

Speaking of the stars, how many hotels have you stayed in that offer views of the night sky anywhere near comparable to those you will be treated to at sea? The farther the ship sails away from land, the clearer the sky will become, as you will leave light pollution behind and experience the most awe-inspiring starry nights you have ever seen. Meanwhile, rather than being disturbed by the noise from the other guests in your hotel, the only sounds you will hear will be those of the sea lapping gently against your ship.

Cross-ocean cruise travel has become a popular alternative to flying to or from a destination as well. I speak from experience when I tell you that my wife and I prefer to sail from the United States to Europe, stay in Europe for a while, and then seek a cruise that will return us to the United States. Even if you are planning a visit to a Caribbean, Mexican, or Central American resort for a week, why not consider simply flying or driving to Fort Lauderdale and taking a seven-day cruise that will give you a chance to visit anywhere from four to six different islands, all with beaches of their own?

How About Your Own Private Island?

JUST IN CASE a luxury hotel delivering you to a series of ports full of relaxing, fun, and memorable adventures isn't enough to entice, consider that some cruise lines own private islands at which they will anchor and offer "tender" service for a day of fun and beach activities.

Carnival Cruise Lines, for instance, not only owns the ships which bear its name. It also owns the ships that sail under the names Princess Cruises, Holland America, Costa Cruises, Cunard, Seaborn, and P&O Cruises, complete with a host of company-owned islands at which each of these lines often stop. Royal Caribbean owns its own line plus Celebrity Cruise Line and the associated islands. Norwegian Cruise Line owns all Norwegian Line vessels and the higher-end lines which sail as Oceania Cruises and Regent Seven Seas.

The private islands in question bear names like Castaway Cay, owned by Disney Cruises, or Half Moon Cay, owned by Holland America. How about Coco Cay, owned and operated by Royal Caribbean? Not surprisingly, Princess Cruises owns an island called Princess Cay. Rounding out the cast of private islands are Great Stirrup Cay and Harvest Caye, both owned by Norwegian Cruise Company.

Each of these islands is located in or near the Bahama Islands, not far off the east coast of the southern United States. They're a great place to begin a cruise so that passengers can acclimate to the sun in the early part of their travels. They're also a great place to end a cruise so that passengers can wind down before nearing the journey's final destination.

A typical day at one of these private islands begins when the ship anchors and the lifeboats are lowered into the water to serve as ferry boats, known as tenders, to transport passengers the short distance from the ship to the island. Soon after breakfast, many guests will return to their stateroom and change into beach attire. They will pack a small tote or backpack with sunscreen, a long-sleeve shirt and a hat to protect from the rays of the sun, a book or magazine, a couple bottles of water, sunglasses, and whatever else comes to mind. After making their way to the tender, they will join others looking to enjoy a day away from the ship on a pristine beach that extends as far as the eye can see.

Early arrival at these private islands is usually a good idea, as it better ensures that you will locate a lounging spot that suits your needs, possibly under a tree that will afford shade when desired and a lounge chair not too far down the beach from where the tender docks. Post-COVID, an early start is likely to be even more important, as the more rigorous health-screening process is likely to create waiting lines.

After settling into your chosen spot, you will find your gaze drawn toward the shoreline, where the turquoise color of the water and the ability to see the sand below will most likely prompt a stroll in that direction to test the temperature of the water and perhaps encourage you to wade in for a swim. Tropical waters are so inviting that people who rarely do more than get their feet wet are often motivated to dive in head-first, even if only for a short time.

While you're relaxing on a chair or blanket, a beach attendant will soon appear and ask if you would like something from the bar or a snack from the restaurant. You won't need cash or a credit card, as your cruise card will be sufficient to settle your account.

As the morning wears on, you may wish to rent a jet ski, take a ride on a glass-bottomed boat, or even head to a cove for some snorkeling. Some passengers will spend the entire day on the island, while others may choose to return to the ship for lunch. Others will enjoy lunch at one of the tiki bars on the island and then return aboard after visiting some of the shops operated by island natives, where handmade items are available for purchase. To pay for these items, you will usually need cash or a credit card, as the shops are not owned by the cruise company.

As I write this chapter, I am envisioning myself sitting on the sand and wishing we had a private island stop built into this cruise. Not all cruises will make a stop like this, but now that we are living in a post-COVID world, cruise lines are putting these islands to even better use. More cruises than ever before are stopping at these private, more contained (and therefore more controllable in terms of sanitation and distancing) islands. In the future, as Nelly suggested, I project that some cruise lines will even consider building cabins on these islands, designed to accommodate overnight stays for many of the passengers who wish to enjoy a bonfire and a night under the stars before returning to the ship.

It isn't difficult to imagine that itineraries might be revised to make these island visits two days instead of one. Would it not, after all, make for an excellent way to enhance social distancing both aboard the ship and on the islands? Would it not also relieve the ship itself of the concern of overcrowding in the dining room or theater? And would it not also afford the crew more unimpeded time to better clean and sanitize the ship?

At the time of this writing, we do not yet have full answers to these questions, but I'm certainly not the first person to consider these possibilities. Until you visit one of these islands yourself, you simply can't appreciate how beautiful they are. They also offer immense capacity for creative additions to an already wonderful cruise vacation.

The concept makes sense even beyond a post-COVID view of cruise vacationing. After all, would you rather attend a luau around the ship's swimming pool or on a pristine island where you can stray a bit from fellow travelers? Have you considered taking a midnight swim under the stars, where the only sounds you'll hear are the sounds of nature? Is waking up in the morning and taking a walk or jog along the water's edge while the sun rises before your eyes something that appeals to you?

At the end of the day, new cruise practices and safety measures will go a long way toward not just enhancing security and passenger wellbeing, but also improving the quality of the vacations themselves. Cruising in a post-COVID world will be better than it ever was before.

And we're just getting started! We haven't even explored the many amenities and offerings that have always been available on cruise vacations and will only be improved moving forward. I don't know about you, but I'm getting a bit hungry as I think on this subject. I'd say it's time to get to the bottom of everything we've been enjoying on our first post-COVID cruise.

Part 2:

THE NITTY GRITTY

4
Sir, Would You Like Pancakes with Your Butter?

WE COULD START our journey into post-COVID cruise features by exploring the cabins, pools, entertainment venues, or amenities. But let's be honest. Some of us are just here for the food and drinks. Whether you select your cruise based on customer reviews of the cuisine or you think of these world-class meals as merely ancillary to the fun, nothing separates a great cruise from just a good one quite like the quality—or for that matter, the quantity—of the food.

"I'll have three scrambled eggs, bacon and sausage, home fries, and a stack of pancakes. And please bring another tub of butter. This one's running low."

This actual breakfast order came from my good friend Doug, whose passion for cruising nearly matched my own, but whose passion for cruise dining, if anything, was far surpassing. An insurance man by trade, Doug always seemed to know more about the dining venues and menus of the world's various cruise lines and ships than he knew about annuities, whole life insurance, or homeowner policies.

On the few cruises where I had the privilege to accompany Doug and his wife Cathy, I often found myself awed by how hard he vacationed. If the ship offered rock climbing, Doug would climb. If there was a scuba-diving excursion, Doug would dive. If the ship had a surfing pool, Doug would surf. Whenever he found an open food venue, Doug would eat—and was he ever good at eating. You could always count on him to order enough to fill multiple plates. When the pancakes arrived, he would lather them up with a mountain of butter so high that the syrup would erupt onto the plate like a sticky Vesuvius.

To bring an appetite of this level to every meal on a cruise ship requires a certain amount of stamina. Over the course of a day aboard ship, the average person will spend approximately five hours at one of the dining venues, a timeframe spread across breakfast, lunch, and dinner while also squeezing in a midmorning snack, afternoon tea, a bedtime treat, and how about a chocolate chip cookie at 2:00 a.m.?

Most cruises offer an array of cuisines, much of it available at all hours of the day and night. Whether you prefer to order your pancakes with a side of butter or vice versa, you will have to work awfully hard to go hungry. My personal preference is for high quality over mass quantity, though I wouldn't classify myself as a food snob. Even if you classify yourself differently, there will be food—of the exceptional type, of the no frills type, and of everything in between—to satisfy you. Just try to keep up with the sheer volume of it.

Breakfast Is for Everyone

SINCE MOST OF us begin the day with breakfast, let's start there. If you're a coffee, juice, and cereal kind of person, you don't even need to leave your cabin, as most cruise lines will deliver this level of fare to any stateroom as early as 6:00 a.m. and as late as 10:00 a.m. The only catch is, you have to fill out the menu left in your room before you retire for the evening and then leave that menu outside your door. Remember to do this, and your food will arrive the next morning at almost precisely the time you indicate on the menu. Nothing makes a person feel quite so much like a monarch as the ability to, with a few strokes of the pen, summon food at an appointed hour.

If planning ahead isn't your thing, and neither is waking up at a specific time, there's always the breakfast buffets. Typically, the buffet restaurants will serve the morning fare between 6:00 a.m. and 10:30 a.m. If you leave one of these places unsatisfied, then you have very exotic tastes indeed. It is difficult to imagine a scenario where there will not be something to satisfy you from any and every food group known to humankind.

Do you desire steak and eggs? A made-to-order omelet whose makeup you personally ordain? Lox or herring with all the add-ons? Waffles of both the Belgian and non-Belgian variety?[1] Fruits from far-flung locales? How about every style of baked goods ever conceived since the dawn of agriculture, from toast to bagels, to donuts, to pastries? If the answer is *yes* to any of these questions, then you will never be disappointed.

Let's say for the sake of argument that you enjoy waking up to the sunrise, or perhaps to an alarm, and arriving for the first meal of the day at a specific time. For you, there is the main dining room. The hours are typically more limited than with room service or the buffet, but in exchange you get to eat with fine silverware, dab at your lips with linen napkins, smooth your hands across a linen tablecloth, and be waited on by a small army of well-groomed servers. The menu won't compare to the buffet in terms of amplitude of selection, but even the pickiest of eaters are still sure to find something that will help them start the day on a full tank.

---

1 Fun fact about Belgian waffles: in Belgium, they call them Brussels waffles.

Maybe you've chosen to book a higher-end suite. For reasons unrelated to the drinks you enjoyed last night, maybe you wake up in a mood that suggests you would be better off avoiding large crowds. Luckily for you, your cruise might offer people in your specific situation a continental breakfast served in a lounge reserved for suite guests. Or you could visit a specialty restaurant where you may order and eat in a more private setting. If you booked a mega-suite, you may have your butler set the dining table in your living room, where he will serve you just about anything available anywhere on the ship.

Clearly Doug favored the buffet, you're thinking. Not so! More often than not, my old friend preferred the dining room for breakfast. Often, he would arrive for breakfast having already warmed up his palate either with room service or a casual grazing through the buffet. In the dining room, Doug was in his glory. He would begin his meal with juice and coffee, but before the main course, he would scarf fresh fruit and oatmeal and/or cereal. He would pull the bread basket close, work over the butter tubs, and even sample a pastry or two before the waiter had even taken his order.

Every cruise the world over adheres to an unwritten policy that your waiter will bring you anything and everything you choose to order from the menu. You want bacon and eggs? "Excellent choice, madam." You want bacon and eggs, potato latkes with applesauce, eggs Benedict, oh, and also a short stack of pancakes, the quiche special, and how about just everything on the left side of the menu? "Right away, sir." Doug was quite skilled at availing himself of this unwritten policy.

Yes, It's Already Time to Eat Again

ASSUMING YOU HAVE taken advantage of the many activities aboard the ship designed to help you work up a fresh appetite, you might actually be hungry by the time 11:30 a.m. or noon rolls around. That is usually when passengers begin to fill the many food venues open for service. If you would rather remain near the pool, you may opt to order a burger or other grilling standard without even having to change from your bathing suit. You will just have to get up from your lounge chair to dine at one of the nearby dining tables.

Unless you arrive near opening time, finding a table in the buffet may prove challenging—particularly on sea days, when passengers flock to this venue in large numbers and practically mob the lunch choices. It is usually worth it to brave the crowd because if you thought the breakfast offerings were unlimited, then you ain't seen nothing yet.

Good luck choosing between at least three different meat dishes, one or two seafood options, myriad pastas and stir-fries, and the enormous variety of soups. Mind you, these are just the hot foods. If you're a sandwich person, they will have you covered. You might also choose from a variety of cold cut meats to eat with the varied assortment of greens available at the salad bar.

Nearby, you will also find a counter displaying a half-dozen or more dessert choices. Never far away will be the ice cream station, where an attendant will load you up with just about any dessert topping you can imagine. If you're having trouble locating the ice cream station, just ask any child. He or she has already performed diligent reconnaissance on this location and will be more than capable of showing you the way.

Some—though certainly not most—passengers prefer to take their lunch in the dining room. Similarly to breakfast, here you can expect a more refined experience with a slightly less abundant menu. You can select a table to share with friends or you can dine alone. Whatever your party, the dining room may be just what you require to enjoy a quiet conversation or to plan the remainder of your day. While you do all this, waiters and wine stewards will take your order and serve you.

As it happened, on that day when Doug ordered his volcano of buttered pancakes, I didn't see him at lunch. Though I couldn't be sure exactly where he ate lunch that day, I could be sure that he ate it somewhere. The answer came later that afternoon, when I ran into him after he had just finished shooting baskets on the sports deck.

"I didn't leave time for lunch," he explained. "So I just settled for a pepperoni pizza and a beer on the way back to my cabin to get my sneakers."

He was off to the next activity already. I trailed after him.

"Where are we eating dinner tonight?" he asked once I had caught up.

I had known Doug long enough by then to understand that this decision had already been made. "Wherever you choose is fine with me."

"Let's meet at the sports bar at 5:30 for cocktails and a game of Trivial Pursuit before dinner."

"Excellent."

"Wear a jacket."

"A jacket?"

"A sport coat. We're going to the steakhouse after cocktails."

When You Just Need a Snack

IF THE HOURS between breakfast and lunch, between lunch and dinner, and between dinner and sleep prove interminable, don't worry; you won't go hungry. In addition to the three main meals of the day, you will be able to find food on your cruise at just about any hour of the day or night.

For that smoky flavor, the pool grill is usually open from 11:00 a.m. to 5:00 or 6:00 p.m. The ice cream stand tends to stay open well into the evening hours. Room service, with its fairly generous menu, is typically open until at least midnight. On some cruises, it's open the full 24/7.

Afternoon tea is still quite popular with Europeans and those of us of a certain age. No matter your age, you will find enough calories served in the designated lounge at 3:00 p.m. each afternoon to assure that you will maintain your body weight and then some. If your body can take it, if you stay up late enough, and if you're willing to wander a little, you're sure to find light fare served somewhere on board well into the night.

The High Point

FOR MANY GUESTS, dinner on a cruise ship represents the high point of the day—and with good reason. Dinner is where a cruise company can truly set itself apart from the competition.

Increasingly over the past decade, cruise companies have begun to offer a number of specialty restaurants ranging from steakhouses to French bistros, Italian trattorias, and locations specializing in Asian cuisines. These restaurants tend to book up early in any cruise, so the sooner you make a reservation after first boarding the ship, the more likely it is that you will be accommodated at the time and place you favor. Most often, you will run into a small upcharge added to your account for dining in one of these venues, but most guests view the charge as plenty worthwhile.

Every few nights on a cruise, my wife and I will opt to change our routine from dining in the buffet or main dining room and visit a specialty restaurant. Whenever we enter a French bistro, we feel as though we have left the ship for a night in Paris. Through the bright lighting emanating from the crystal chandeliers, we enjoy the beautiful tapestries adorning the walls and the flowers strategically placed around the room. We take our seats on French provincial chairs and ease into the soft music played by a violinist strolling through the room. Distinctly French fare dominates the menu, though most specialty restaurants offer a number of food items for the less adventurous. Be certain to leave room for Cherries Jubilee as you sip a wonderful glass of Bordeaux.

At Doug's request, next we venture to the steakhouse for surf and turf or a sumptuous bone-in ribeye. The mood in these establishments is one of darkened candlelight and posh velour or leather seating. There's usually a table set with a cascade of wine glasses and varied silverware for every course, typically beginning with shrimp cocktail, escargot, and onion soup. Next comes the Caesar salad prepared tableside with a glass of fine red or white wine. Tonight, my entrée will be the veal chop or maybe the rack of lamb. Doug, always on his best behavior in these specialty restaurants, will not skip a course. He will only order one item per course in this setting—at least until dessert, when the gloves come off.

Not to slight the other specialty restaurants, you will be equally pleased to dine in the Italian trattoria with its checkered tablecloths, straw-covered wine bottles, and waiters dressed in attire similar to what you might encounter in Venice or Rome. Speaking of the former, odds are decent that you will spot a gondola on display. Whatever the décor, the room will certainly bring the distinct aroma of garlic to make you feel like you're in Italy. A formidable assortment of olive oils will complement your choice of appetizer, salad, and third (and possibly fourth) course. Pasta and cheese options will be unlimited. I recommend the Braciole, an Italian favorite.

Becoming more and more popular on more and more ships are the Asian cuisines inspired by the spicy sweetness of Thai, the curry of Indian, and/or the assorted flavors of Vietnamese. Menus always feature at least some influence from Chinese and Japanese cuisine. If you enjoy sushi and spring rolls, you will have your fill. No need to worry if you are out of practice with chopsticks, for all you have to do is ask for a knife and fork.

Between the post-COVID demand for more private and distanced dining experiences and the good old-fashioned imperative for cruise ships to leverage advantage over the competition, we will no doubt see more specialty restaurants emerge in the coming years. English pubs, Mexican taquerias, New Orleans Cajun-style eateries—as long as food choice and variety are a prime concern for passengers, cruise companies will continue to evolve and expand.

The specialty restaurants on a cruise ship are certainly special, but the main dining room will always be the place where most passengers choose to enjoy their evening meal. Ships will continue to offer early and late seatings in the dining room in a post-COVID world, but there is another trend that I expect to see expanding in the coming months and years, if only to accommodate the need for social distancing. That trend is anytime dining. This feature allows you the option to be seated in the dining room at a time you preselect. What makes this particularly attractive is that you can schedule your own dining time, you can sit with whomever you choose, and it is likely to thin out the herds, so to speak, during the typical early and late seatings in the formal dining rooms.

As well behaved as Doug was at the steakhouse, the same cannot be said of his almost regular appearances in the main dining room. I truly believe that if Doug could have arranged it, he would have asked to be seated for both the early and the late seatings each and every night. To make up for this lost opportunity, Doug would usually order more than one meal during his scheduled seating. We learned this almost right away—on the second night of our first cruise with Doug and Cathy—when our extremely helpful server moved our party of four to a table for six to accommodate the number of plates Doug required to complete his meal.

Unlike the specialty restaurants, the main dining room is not equipped to cook every dish to order. The menu is diverse and the options will include all food groups, but the preparation and delivery of food will be what you might expect at a wedding or banquet. The sheer number of patrons necessitates this format. That said, the quality will be high. It is simply that the meal may lack the same level of intimacy or variety you can expect at the specialty restaurants. My wife and I have enjoyed many meals in the dining room at a table for two. On other occasions, we have elected to dine with people we met along the journey.

The final option for dinner is the evening buffet, which will offer everything being served in the main dining room with very few exceptions. Many more passengers than you might think will choose this venue for dinner because of its casual atmosphere and the ability to eat only what you choose to put on your plate. For some, this means a decidedly lighter meal than you might receive in the dining room. For others, it's just the opposite, as the buffet nature of the arrangement allows you to pile your plate as high as you like and return as many times as your stomach can bear it.

The buffet is also a nice option for three scenarios you might not initially think about:

1) When an excursion or a plan to visit one of the ship's many amenities or shows prevents you from taking advantage of either the early or late seating time in the formal dining room.
2) When you have somehow forgotten to eat during traditional dinner hours, it's late, and you're still hungry enough for a full meal.
3) When the ship has scheduled a night where formal attire is encouraged in the dining room and you prefer to keep things casual.

My wife and I have certainly been there before—it's formal night and suddenly you don't love the idea of returning to your cabin to get dressed to the nines. These things happen. When they do, we will select the buffet as a courtesy to those who have decided to dress for the occasion.

I never did ask Doug why he preferred the dining room to the buffet for most of his meals, and I regret not doing so, given that we have encountered a fairly sizable number of Dougs in the buffet on the many cruises we have taken. Incidentally, Dougs come in all sizes and genders. On more than one occasion, I have had to step out of the way of a young, female Doug (one who could not have weighed more than ninety pounds) as she tight-roped down the aisle in search of her table, three overloaded plates balanced precariously down her arm. We have witnessed people of all sizes returning to the buffet counter as many as four or five times, each time wandering back with what might well fill an entire football team. I have no right to point fingers. On lobster night, I eat in the buffet so that no one will notice how many lobster tails I can devour in one sitting.

In this sense, Doug surely would have felt right at home in the buffet, but I somehow think he enjoyed the faces of the waiters whenever he ordered several meals simultaneously in the dining room. He certainly gave the crew members something to talk about at the end of their evening shifts.

I will close this section with a final salute to Doug, my great friend, who, even ten years after his death, has managed to help me write about the food venues you will find on your next cruise. Contrary to what you might think, Doug did not pass away due to his legendary diet. In fact, he stayed mostly fit and active throughout his life. Sadly, following a hip surgery when he was in his mid-sixties, he contracted a terrible blood disorder and an infection that ultimately took his life. I still miss him, just as the dining room waiters on a number of cruises do as well.

Let's All Have a Drink

IN MY YOUNGER years, I enjoyed watching Dean Martin perform. He would sit on a stool center stage with a drink in his hand, and between the love songs he sang, he would pause to banter with his friends from the Rat Pack, who also tended to enjoy a drink or two on stage. Great comedians like George Carlin built their acts around looking three sheets to the wind, or at least still hungover from the previous night. The sit-com "Cheers" ushered a similar spirit onto millions of television screens once per week through most of the '80s.

Back then, the term "designated driver" was less common, the bars stayed open past 4:00 a.m., and "Uber" was still just the German word for "over." By and large, people these days are more responsible with their drinking and commuting. If you partake of alcoholic beverages, this is another advantage of cruise vacations, as you get to enjoy a period where you never much have to worry about the commute part. It's a little like being Dean Martin.

After you walk up the gangway, you may, if you so choose, commence drinking. You can put your car keys in a safe place in your cabin, as you won't need them again until your vacation is over. Allow the captain and his/her staff of officers to do all the driving for you for a while. They will steer the vessel from port to port while you and your companions enjoy every minute of the voyage.

It could be that, in your opinion, part of that enjoyment will include sipping your favorite cocktail, beer, or glass of wine. If so, take comfort in the knowledge that you will never be at a loss to locate a bar or lounge to serve you at all hours of the day and night, and you will never even once have to worry about how you will get yourself home.

One of the fun things about the first day of your cruise is that a bar steward will likely greet you with a glass of champagne, mimosa, or other cocktail just as soon as you step off the gangway and onto the ship—you know, to help get the travel dust out of your throat. You hardly even had to work to get your hands on your first drink of the cruise and now you can take it with you all over the ship. I recommend enjoying it as you wander around marveling at said ship's beauty.

During your exploration, whenever your glass runs dry, you won't have to go far to find a refill, as you will pass any number of bars and lounges open for business. If you choose to sit poolside and rest for a few minutes, a steward will see you and ask if he or she may bring you something to drink.

When you enter your stateroom to unpack, you might find your attention drawn to the mini refrigerator stocked with small bottles of spirits and several cans of beer. Next to your telephone, you will discover a list of numbers to call for service. If you dial the one that says "room service," a cheerful person on the other end of the line will ask if you would like a snack or something to drink. You can even order your favorite brand of beverage, which will be delivered in no time at all.

Once you have freshened up and are ready to head out for what most cruise lines refer to as the sail-away party on one of the open decks, you are certain to pass a bar or lounge, or maybe even more than one. Stop in to whichever one appeals to you, provided you are up for afternoon or pre-dinner cocktails. My personal preference is to explore all the venues over the course of the cruise—and there are usually quite a few of them. I recognize, however, that some guests are creatures of habit who prefer to stick to a specific lounge or bar on a more regular basis.

If you enjoy a martini, you will likely find a bar whose name contains some application of the word "martini." Whatever the establishment's name, the bartender will be well versed in the art of mixology, able to mix any and every drink you have heard of and even a few you haven't. On our first day on any ship, my wife and I like to explore a bit before settling on a favorite spot to enjoy our pre-dinner cocktails. Our ultimate selection usually has a lot to do with the personality of the man or woman tending the bar. Over the years, we have come to realize that a good bartender is almost as important as a good cabin steward.

You won't need to worry about going thirsty once the dinner hour arrives either. Soon after being seated and greeted by your waiter, a wine steward will appear at your table and ask if you and your companions would like a glass or bottle of wine. The steward will also be happy to refresh your cocktail of choice. It matters not at all if you have chosen to dine in the buffet restaurant instead of the main dining room, as bar stewards will be circulating through the buffet as well.

After dinner, you may find yourself heading to the theater to take in the evening's main show, a lounge to check out a comedian's set, a more intimate musical performance, or maybe even a magic show. Depending on the number of lounges your ship offers, your choices could be many, and the quality of entertainment will always be high. Wherever you land, you will be able to order your after-dinner drink of choice as stewards work through the theater and lounges. It's not unlike Las Vegas.

As the evening progresses, certain lounges convert to dance venues with music played for passengers of all ages and preferences. Of course, there is always alcohol to help keep you moving. If you opt for the casino, you may rest assured that adult beverages are available at the casino bar, which may double as the on-ship sports bar. If you gamble enough, the pit boss may even offer you a drink on the house.

Likely all of this, coupled with the sounds of the sea

and the gentle breezes the ship creates as it glides through the water, will at some point send you into a deep and proper sleep back in your cabin. The next day, you will awaken fresh(ish) and ready to plan your next adventure aboard the vessel. It is best practice to dedicate your first day (which is almost always spent fully at sea) to getting better acquainted with the ship. If you are inclined, you can do this with a Bloody Mary, a mimosa, or any other standard-issue morning-time adult beverage of choice.

By lunchtime, the pool bar will be hopping. So will the bar stewards, who will eagerly traverse the pool area with a tray in hand. It is not an uncommon sight, no matter where you look, to find groups of people enjoying a drink as they converse, engage in a game of cards, or read a book in the panoramic lounge overlooking the front of the ship. Variations of this sight will pop up at regular intervals over the course of that first day and well into the week, where you will encounter any number of new settings at which to drink, both on ship and at the various off-ship stops.

You will see a large number of drinkers and drinking styles as well. One morning, my wife and I were getting ready to leave the ship to join a tour when we overheard a man and woman engaged in a rather heated discussion.

"Get out of the seat and get moving with me to the gangway or we're going to miss the tour," the woman said.

"I'm not going anywhere except right here," the gentleman countered. "I paid for the bar package, and I'm going to enjoy it."

"It's 8:00 a.m. and you're already on your second Bloody whatever-you-call-it."

"If you think I'm losing this seat, which might not be available when we return, you've lost your mind."

Who's Paying for All Those Drinks?

THAT RATHER DETERMINED gentleman raises a point. Hopefully, you don't get all the way through your first day on the ship before you realize that you have to pay for these drinks somehow.

How you opt to pay is another matter. Cruise lines offer a variety of ways to enjoy adult beverages. You may pay as you go—the option I prefer, if for no other reason than that my liver is no longer as young as it used to be. You may purchase an all-inclusive bar package before you leave home or at any time once the voyage has begun. Friends who have chosen the package swear by it. As they tell it, they didn't come on vacation to be constantly signing bar chits. Others use it as an excuse to step out from their normal routine at home. One thing that's certain about the bar package is that the purchaser will drink more, and not less, as the trip continues.

Some cruise companies take the choice away completely by offering unlimited drinks at no additional cost when you book your cruise. Unless you are a bit naïve, you will realize that the cost of beverages has already been built into the price you have paid for the cruise. That said, it is nice to know that you won't have to worry about running up a large bar bill that will have to be settled at the end of the cruise.

Of course, if you are among those who don't enjoy (or choose not to drink) alcoholic beverages, you won't be forced to make these decisions. But you will do yourself a favor by asking your booking agent if there is an alternate price for your cruise if you opt out of the all-inclusive offering. Sometimes these cruise lines bake the price of alcohol into the rate and you have to ask for the non-alcoholic rate directly.

More important to all of us who consume alcoholic beverages should be the question of what it is we're getting for our money. If we buy the package, are we getting well brands or premium brands? Are gratuities included, or will they be added to our bill? Is there a limit on the number of drinks we can order each day? Is the $200 bottle of wine or champagne part of the package? The wise consumer will seek answers to these questions before committing to any prepaid package.

Meanwhile, for those of us who choose to pay as we go, the price we are asked to pay for a drink sometimes may cause us to wonder if we made the right choice. Whenever I'm served a less-than-full glass of wine and later peruse the chit, I will wonder whether I have made a mistake or the bartender has rung up someone else's drink on my bill.

It is almost enough to make you appreciate the appeal of sober cruising, as will some of the other patrons you might encounter late at night. On exactly such an occasion, when my wife and I were asleep, we heard a knock on our stateroom door.

"Honey!" came the voice. "I can't find my key. Please open the door and let me in."

I don't know who *honey* was, but I do know that she was neither me nor my wife.

"Please, honey! I've only had a couple drinks. I promise not to snore."

Whatever your preference, have fun on your cruise vacation. Enjoy all it has to offer, including the outrageously fine and abundant dining and drinking options. They are sure to provide you with the fuel you need for all your on-ship and off-ship adventures. I promise we will get to those adventures. First, though, now that you're all full of food and drink, let's figure out where you can rest and relax.

5
Where to Sleep and Where to Relax

LET'S TALK CABINS and staterooms, because as easy as it was to find food and drink aboard your ship, selecting where to sleep and relax might prove a bit more challenging. There are so many options to choose from, in so many differing price ranges, that it is wise to give this a lot of thought before you book your cruise. This is particularly true post-pandemic, as the need for social distancing and increased sanitization efforts may or may not compel you to spend more time in your room than you might have in the past.

First, some clarification on the terms at play. The words "cabin" and "stateroom" mean the same thing. It's really just a matter of how much you want to class up the discussion. The latter term sounds a little more aristocratic. Some people prefer it. After all, they're on this vacation to feel like royalty, so they might as well use words fit for royalty. Me? I use them interchangeably and will continue to do so over the course of this discussion.

On any cruise ship in the world, cabins range in size from quite small with no view to outrageously opulent with views in all directions from a private balcony. Between these extremes, you will find no fewer than a half-dozen other choices, each level offering a different balance of space, view, and amenities. Which level you choose depends entirely on your personal preferences and the requirements of your traveling party.

Our food-fiend friend Doug and his wife, for instance, would spend so much time on social and physical activities on the ship and at ports of call that they preferred not to dedicate too much money to their sleeping space. For them, the lower-priced, smaller, windowless cabins in the center of the ship made the most sense. While I understood the logic, the logistics always baffled me. Doug was no small fellow, so I always had a hard time imagining how the two of them could navigate a small room with no view and a bathroom the size of a broom closet.

"We're on a budget," Doug once told me. "I'd rather spend my money on seeing the sights and enjoying a few cocktails."

I can attest to his appetite for these things.

"But don't you like being able to spend some time in a private, comfortable space once in a while?" I asked. "Somewhere to kick up your legs?"

"I get where you're coming from. But we only use the cabin to dress, shower, and sleep. I didn't sign up to stay in the room. So why spend extra for more space when there's always something going on around the ship?"

Strong points all around. I will admit that the inside staterooms aren't exactly floating prison cells. They're always attractively decorated, clean as a whistle, and a lot less expensive than what my wife and I prefer. Then again, we crave a little sunlight and a shower large enough that we don't have to work ourselves into pretzels to fit into it. I'm no little fellow either. In my view, if I'm on a luxury vacation, I want every part of it to feel luxurious, including the sleeping and showering situations.

If you are considering an inside cabin, rest assured that you will have plenty of amenities to meet the basic needs. There will be a television mounted on the wall and a small desk for writing (though don't expect enough space to scribble your thoughts for a book while you avoid interruptions from Nelly). In any case, the desk will serve as sufficient space to set up your tablet or laptop. Shower-wise, maybe you're smaller or more flexible than I am, or maybe you don't mind roughing it on the hygiene front for a week. Or if you apply a little ingenuity, you might find that the showers in the locker room attached to the fitness center are not a bad choice for taking care of your hygiene needs.

Similar to the inside staterooms are the outside cabins. They're usually about the same size and come with the same amenities, the main difference being that the outside cabins add the feature of a sea view from the four-foot-by-four-foot picture window that has replaced the small round porthole of yesteryear on most ships. Given the arguably scant nature of this upgrade, the increase in price to secure one of these rooms is usually pretty modest. Still, most passengers agree that the mere presence of the window brightens the room during daylight hours and tends to remove the sense of claustrophobia one might experience in a windowless space.

If you are considering either of these options, it's important that you don't ignore the deck on which your stateroom will reside. The lower you are in the ship, the farther you will be from the most appealing venues. Even though the main dining room and the theater are usually on lower decks, most everything else you will be drawn to is closer to the top of the ship. Also, some still say that the lower levels reduce the sensation of sea movement, even though modern stabilizers have nearly eliminated the feel of the ocean swaying beneath your feet. In any case, if you're prone to motion sickness, lower levels might be a safer bet. Don't pass on the window either, as being able to see the horizon at all times tends to help with seasickness as well.

Next up the list of upgrades is the balcony. For another modest increase in price, you can select a stateroom that allows you a small private balcony. The size of these rooms and the amenities will not differ substantially from the two previous categories, but the ability to slide open your glass door and step outside to feel and smell the fresh sea air will more than make up for the fact that you are still only in a fifteen-foot-by-fifteen-foot room. Having that outdoor space will make the place feel twice as large.

Even before COVID, these cabins had become so popular among cruise-goers that many cruise lines eliminated the ocean-view cabins completely and replaced them with balcony staterooms. Post-COVID, when social distancing will require the staggering of events, public spaces, and meals, having that space to chill outside will become even more appealing.

If you are among the many who lean in this direction, just don't get caught napping, as the balcony staterooms will be among the first to sell out once the cruise has been advertised and becomes available for booking. Make sure to be ready as soon as the countdown ends and you're allowed to book your stateroom, and take comfort in the notion that the small added cost is almost certain to be worth it. The first time you sit on your private outdoor chairs next to the small table set between them, sipping a cocktail or eating your breakfast, you will be glad you upgraded your cabin.

Most of the staterooms on nearly every ship at sea fall into one of the three categories above, but most ships offer further upgrades to discuss. Typically, the term used for the rooms in these categories is "suite." There are myriad suite options that vary from cruise line to cruise line, so if you like shopping in the luxury category, it's usually a good idea to shop around.

No matter what your budget, there are options that will enable you to enjoy your cruise without having to take out a second mortgage. Once you board, almost everything available to the Rockefellers of the world will be available to you and me. We will eat in the same restaurants, swim in the same pools, and sit next to each other (six feet apart, of course) in the same theaters during the shows. We may not have a butler attending us directly, but let's just call that "roughing it."

As you consider your cabin selection, don't overlook the importance of the human beings who will be joining you on this cruise. You weren't planning on leaving your kids at home, were you? Okay, maybe you were. But if you do want to bring them (or even if you don't want to bring them but have to), their presence will surely impact the selection. The same can be said for traveling with your extended family or a set/network of friends.

In any case, a family with two or more children will have to make choices to accommodate everyone. Couples traveling with a baby will have needs of their own.

Like Nell, Nancy, and Marie, three women cruising together will have decisions to make as well. I should ask them what choices they made the next time I see them out and about.

Confession is Good for the Soul

OKAY, FINE. If truth be known, my wife and I do occasionally book a suite on a cruise vacation. The older I get, the more frequent this choice becomes. For many years of cruising, we availed ourselves of the smaller cabins, and we never felt we had been slighted of a great vacation because of our choice. Since most of our cruises these days are of longer duration with more days fully at sea, we use our cabin for greater portions of the time.

For instance, many afternoons we will sit out on the more spacious balconies off these suites, gazing at the water and/or reading a book. We sometimes watch a movie on the high-definition television now available in every stateroom. Every once in a while, we will order dinner and enjoy it in our suite. Sometimes, we invite another couple we met on the ship to join us for a cocktail on our balcony. For us, it is worth the extra cost, as cruising has become a big part of our way of life.

Wait. Here comes Nelly now. I should ask her how she and her friends have arranged their cabins. I'll pause the writing now and report back shortly.

...

"**Nell!**" **I said** when I spotted her power-walking past the pool. "How's everything going? I've been meaning to ask you about what accommodations you and your girlfriends selected for this cruise."

"That's a fairly personal question," Nelly said with a smirk. "I thought you were a happily married man. Perhaps I misjudged you."

I chuckled it off. "No, you didn't misjudge me. I apologize if I seemed too forward, but I'm asking in support of my book about cruise vacations. I'm working on a chapter about the different cabin arrangements guests might make. It occurred to me that I have no direct experience with how you're traveling."

"In style!" she quipped.

"No, I mean in a party of three friends."

"If it gets me in the book, I'll tell you."

"You are already in the book, so what do you have to share?"

Now she grabbed a seat in the nearest poolside lounger and furrowed her brow, all business. "It's varied over the years. On our first adventure, we each booked an inside cabin, just for the sake of privacy. The cost of three cabins wound up being more expensive than if we'd shared a suite. Ever since, we've sampled suites of different sizes with different amenities. Now we go for more space: two bathrooms and a living area where one of us can sleep while the other two convert the king bed to two twins." She held up a finger at me. "Don't get any ideas, as the three of us know how to handle ourselves. We make a formidable team."

With a laugh, I thanked Nell for her input and let her return to her relaxing.

"I'm going to have a ton of great stuff for you when you get to the people-watching chapter," she said.

"Can't wait," I replied, wandering off in search of the ice cream bar.

...

The suites aboard a ship range from what is often termed a "mini-suite" all the way up to the (usually singular) "owner's suite." They vary in size from what may be described as a small apartment to a large, sprawling home. Some mini-suites can list at only a tad more expensive than a balcony cabin. In exchange for the added cost, you can expect an extra hundred or so square feet of living space, a bathtub in the bathroom, and a small sitting area with a couch and one or two chairs. Your balcony will also be a little larger. The mini-suites go by many different names depending on the cruise line, sometimes called veranda suites, sometimes penthouses, sometimes concierge suites, and sometimes signature suites.

Whatever their name, they may offer a few extra amenities as well, such as priority boarding on the day of embarkation and priority exiting at ports of call, a nice amenity indeed. If you or someone you're traveling with plans to do a lot of internet-ing, booking a mini-suite might also entitle you to reduced-price Internet service, which is nice because, depending on your usage levels, Internet access on cruises is often on the expensive side. Further, making a reservation in a specialty restaurant might be easier to accomplish as a mini-suite guest. If you are traveling with a baby or two younger children, the couch which opens to a double bed might come in handy.

Next up the suite-level food chain is a kind of stateroom that might go unnamed. More interesting than what the various cruise lines choose to call these rooms is the description of what 500 square feet of living space gives you on a cruise ship. These suites offer a living area separate from the sleeping area, a large bathroom with two sinks, a shower, and a separate bathtub. The closet is much larger, as is the drawer space. On longer trips, you may find the extra space an inducement to spend more time in the suite.

On many ships, the higher the price and greater the space of your suite, the more considerable the assortment of extras that might make the price differential worthwhile to you. Larger suites often include access to a private lounge, where continental breakfast and a light lunch are offered daily while you read your newspaper or watch television. A concierge will be in attendance to book reservations both on and off the ship, exchange currencies, print boarding passes, and answer any and all of your questions. Some ships offer a private pool area for certain levels of suites.

In more recent offerings, I have noticed a new category called "spa suites." At the time of this writing, my wife and I have not experienced one of these suites firsthand, but they are usually grouped together in an area of the ship that allows easier access to the fitness center, the spa treatment rooms, and to a pool reserved exclusively for this level of suite. If you are interested, ask about this alternative when booking, and your travel agent or cruise consultant will be happy to gather more information.

By now, you may have noticed the pattern. I'm working my way up the ladder of opulence and comfort available to those who are willing to reach into their wallet and pay for the privilege of sailing like a prince or princess. Suites get even sweeter when you consider living spaces of 800, 1,000, 1,200, 2,000 and even 4,000 square feet—all for you and your party. Certainly, these suites serve a utilitarian purpose if you're traveling as a family of six or greater. If you're the CEO of a company who wishes to entertain employees you've invited on this cruise, a large suite serves as an ideal place to entertain your guests (unless of course you are concerned that inviting them into this level of stateroom will make them wonder why you get to sleep in here and they do not).

Okay, I have another confession to make. On a recent pre-pandemic cruise, my wife and I enjoyed a 1,000-square-foot suite. In my defense, how could I write about it if I didn't try it out? Our suite featured a bedroom separated by closed doors from the main living space, where the couch could turn into a bed whenever I started snoring. There was a dining table complete with four chairs, and a media room with a fifty-inch screen to view any of the several hundred movies and documentaries preprogrammed into the entertainment system.

We had two full bathrooms, the smaller one equipped with a sink, shower, and toilet while the master bathroom attached to the bedroom also delivered a whirlpool tub and bidet. The deck was quite spacious, with two lounge chairs, a table large enough for dining with two straight chairs, and of course, a hot tub. Also, yes, this suite did in fact have a butler who stocked our bar and set our table for breakfast and dinner whenever we asked. Everything was so comfortable and luxurious that the captain almost had to summon the police to remove us at the end of the cruise.

By the way, the cost was a lot less than you might imagine, because the cruise took us across the Atlantic with only two ports of call in fourteen days. Pro tip: a greater number of sea days translates to a reduction in the price because of how expensive it is for a ship to dock every day.

I mentioned numbers greater than 1,000 square feet. Maybe someday, my wife and I will see firsthand what a suite of larger size actually looks like in person rather than simply dreaming about them while perusing cruise brochures or sneaking a peak on the last day of a cruise when the suite is being freshened up for the next guest. As the battle for market share continues between cruise lines in the post-COVID world, I can't imagine what additional amenities purchasers of these suites will receive, short of stock ownership in the cruise line itself.

Where to Dip Your Toes

ONE SUNNY AFTERNOON at sea on my first post-COVID cruise, I was sitting poolside reading a thriller when I overheard a voice I will never fail to remember. As she was prone to do, Nell was interviewing random strangers about how they were enjoying their cruise, where they came from, and what motivated them to book a cruise for their vacation.

After her last round of investigative reporting, I caught her attention with a wave.

"Nell!" I said when she came up next to me, casting a shadow over my book. "I see you're meeting new people."

"Always," she said with a wink.

"You know, I've been thinking. How would you like to help me describe what goes on around the pool venues on this ship?"

"You really haven't been pulling my leg, have you? I really am going to be in your book."

With a shrug, I made it clear that there would be no avoiding it. "Here's what I'd like you to do..."

In all honesty, since I don't do a lot of swimming on these vacations, I'd been having difficulty describing the pool venues in a way that would do justice to their beauty and overall importance to a successful cruise experience. I wanted to capture not only the pool in all its glory, but also what motivated people to frequent these venues with such vigorous enthusiasm. It seemed to me that Nell, who could often be found lounging or chatting in the pool areas, would be the perfect person to help bridge the gap. Plus, if she went to work on this task, it would free up some more time for me to relax and enjoy reading a book instead of researching for one.

"Did you see the lady I was just talking to when you called me over?"

"I did. She seemed to be enjoying your conversation."

She looked back over her shoulder as if making sure no one was listening. "Be careful. She's an FBI agent. If she finds out we're planning to use her in our book, we may have a problem."

So my book had just become *our* book. I wondered how Nell would react when she picked up her copy, only to find my name alone on the cover.

"I'll do that, Nell," I said, humoring her. "Thanks for the heads up."

With that, she saluted and headed off to begin her new assignment. As we await her input, I offer my independent thoughts on the subject.

The swimming pool venues on the hundreds of cruise ships circling the globe are always quite different from one another in appearance and features, as they are one of the primary ways for cruise companies to differentiate themselves from the competition. No matter what the cruise line, one thing is for certain. The pools will serve as the centerpiece. They have been the main area of gathering, daytime entertainment, and sun-splashed relaxation on every oceangoing cruise we have taken.

Typically, the main pool sits atop the vessel mid ship, nestled in the two open-air decks that welcome the sun by day and the moon and stars by night. Depending on the capacity of the ship, this pool could be on the smaller side or quite large indeed. Either way, it is always attractively designed while remaining functional. The temperature of the water may depend on many factors, but even on the chilliest cruises, the hot tubs anchoring the pool will always provide a place to warm up after a refreshing swim. On some of the higher-end and/or newer ships, the pool may be equipped with a retractable roof in case of inclement weather.

Surrounding the pool, you will find comfortable lounge chairs for sunbathing or catching up on sleep. Guests will be reading books or magazines, listening to music through their earbuds, working crosswords or Sudoku puzzles, or chatting with the people next to them. You will likely notice that some of the lounges are draped with towels, books, sunglasses, or a small carrying bag but no live human beings. This is how some people reserve their chairs and ensure that no one takes them while they are swimming or paying a visit to the bar, an eatery, or the restroom. While chair-reserving of this nature is essential for these quick trips to and from your poolside space, some people have turned the practice into something more closely resembling chair piracy. More on this later.

Behind the lounge chairs and closer to the sides of the ship, you will find tables and chairs for guests to enjoy lunch or a game of cards while protected from the sun by an overhang from the deck above. At one end of the pool, a bar will be open for business throughout the day and a grilling area will allow passengers to enjoy lunch or a snack poolside without having to change from their bathing suit to enter a dining room.

The swimming venues offer an excellent opportunity for people-watching, a sport that has always interested me. Nell clearly shared my fascination with the subject, though her particular brand of people-watching was more of a contact sport than my own. So completely did she dedicate herself to this task that I didn't see her for the next two days. But when she finally did catch up with me, she brought along a veritable treasure trove of information.

"Where have you been hiding?" I asked. "I thought you'd abandoned our little project." Inwardly I chided myself for using the word "our."

"Well, I had lots of ground to cover." She paused to introduce herself to my wife, who had heard plenty about Nell prior to this moment and looked pleased to finally experience her presence firsthand.

Nell didn't waste another moment. "Did you know there are three pools on this ship? One for families to enjoy, one for people our age where children are discouraged from congregating, and even a smaller pool near the fitness center that I almost didn't find?"

What followed was a briefing on Nell's activities over the past two days, one so detailed that it would have impressed any CEO of any major company in the world so much that he or she would have hired or promoted her on the spot. Although it did get off to a bit of a rocky start...

"First and foremost, we have to talk about what these people wear," she said. "Even before I approached some of them, I had learned a lot about them. One gentleman was wearing a Speedo that left little to the imagination. Too bad you're not writing pornography. He would have made for a strong subject."

While I had anticipated a certain level of fervor from Nell, my first impression was that she had misunderstood the mission slightly. Clearly, she still had a slightly different audience in mind for "our" book.

"That's fine, Nell. But I'm not sure how much space there'll be in this book to cover the subject of swimwear. Some people are less modest than others with their suits; that's true. But what I'm interested in is what you learned about the people themselves. What makes the average pool-goer tick?"

Nell sat on the end of my wife's lounge chair and settled in. "Well, first there's the loners. I began by seeking out people who were sitting all alone by the pool, thinking they would be willing to talk with me. I got a few brush offs, but a number of guests actually seemed pleased to engage in a conversation. I don't want to point but if you look over my left shoulder across the pool, you'll see a beautiful young woman in a pink bikini who looks like she could be Miss America except that she's from the Dominican Republic, so I guess she'd be Miss Dominican Republic."

I casually glanced in that direction. It didn't take long to single out the woman she was referring to—or for that matter, the other beautiful young woman in the lounger next to her. "You certainly know how to pick your interview subjects," I quipped.

"One doesn't speak a word of English, but the other was very helpful in translating and very nice to me. It turns out they're members of the cast that performs in the theater. They're dancers of one sort or another. They said they're working on their tans during their time off."

The notion that cast members would use the pool during the day intrigued me to where I wanted to know more. I didn't press the subject further for fear that Nell—or my wife—might mistake my interest in the bikini-clad interview subjects as something other than research for my non-pornographic book.

"Who else did you meet?" I asked instead.

"This ship is like reading a history book about world travelers," Nell said with wide eyes. "I met a couple from Finland, a single man from Ireland who actually invited me to dinner when he found out I was single and traveling with my girlfriends, and a family with a teenage son and a slightly younger daughter who were from Germany. I'll save the Irishman for last, if you don't mind."

"However you want to proceed, Nell."

Nell blushed a bit but then told me how the family pool was a bit more active with swimmers and games being played and a little too noisy to understand every word of the interviews she conducted. The German family were on vacation with their children, the parents serving as high school teachers in Hamburg. The mother taught English, so she spoke the language beautifully. Her husband was a science teacher with the brainy-guy look to support that career. Their children were polite and seemed to be having a nice time.

"If I had to guess," Nell said, "I'd think the kids would have rather been on a ship with more kids their age than their parents' age."

"Not many kids in the family pool then?"

She explained that the head count of children was lower than expected and the family pool was smaller than the main pool. "Still, the people with families seemed quite content to have a space away from those of us in the more mature stages of life."

"Tell me about the couple from Finland."

"They were more or less our age. How old are you, by the way?"

"I'm seventy-four, so my guess is that you're being extremely charitable by referring to them as 'our' age."

She laughed appreciatively. "I can see what you see in this guy," she joked to my wife. Then she returned to business. "If I had to guess, they come from a bit of money. I could tell just by looking at them that they were people of means and purpose. The husband was extremely handsome and in great shape. He was dressed in a linen shirt, khaki pants, and Gucci shoes with no socks."

"Here we go again with their clothing," I said with a smile. "They don't sound dressed for swimming. I thought you were working the pool areas."

She shrugged. "I got bored and decided to check out a few other places but I'll get back to the pools, I promise. His wife was also dressed to the nines. She had a rigid jaw, but she was very attractive too."

"What did the three of you discuss?"

Nell went on to share what had to have been nearly all of their life story. I could only imagine how exhausted the couple from Finland must have been after Nell finally let them get back to reading their books in a quieter area of the ship.

"Anyway," Nell said, winding down, "they're diplomats of some sort on tour for the Finnish government. They were polite if a bit proper. All in all, I think they found me to be a refreshing change of pace."

Now we had come down to the Irishman. I could sense that Nell was as anxious to tell this part of the story as I was to hear it. She took a deep breath, fluttered her eyes, and couldn't hide her smile as she spoke.

"So you want to hear about Seamus, I suppose."

"Only if you want to share."

"I was scoping out the pool by the fitness center as part of my assignment, and there was this adorable man sitting all alone and reading a book. He smiled at me before I could even approach him."

With a nod, I encouraged her to continue.

"He introduced himself as Seamus O'Reilly from Dublin and asked me my name." She beamed. "We hit it off from the moment I sat next to him. He was soaking wet from a dip in the thermal pool, which if you haven't seen it, it has a rain shower, a whirlpool bench, and steam rising from the surface. Seamus told me he was a poet on vacation by himself, hoping to write some poetry. I must tell you that he was a lot more forthcoming about his work than you've been. I'm afraid I may not have time left to continue helping you."

My wife asked Nelly to dish the details.

"Seamus and I did eventually have dinner together in the cozy Italian restaurant on board. After dinner, we sat by this very pool, enjoying the moon and the stars, and sipped an after-dinner drink."

She went on to describe how the main pool is transformed at night into a destination unlike any other on the ship. There is no hustle and bustle, simply the moon causing the water of the pool to glisten as the warm breezes pass by. She continued her enchanting description of the evening before casually mentioning that Seamus was staying in a beautiful suite with a living room and a balcony that wrapped around the back of the ship.

"I think I should thank you for putting me to work," she said. "Without you prompting me, I might not have met him."

I didn't want to burst her bubble, but having gotten to know Nell, I am certain that she would have engaged Seamus in conversation whether I had put her on assignment or not.

My wife grinned. "Are you going to see him again?"

"Tomorrow, we're going ashore to visit a village he spent time in on a previous tour."

"That sounds nice, Nell," I said. "And I understand if your literary focus has become a little more poetic since the last time we met. But I'm wondering if you could do me one last favor before I lose your services."

She gestured for me to proceed.

"I know you're an early riser," I explained. "I'm wondering if you could meet me here by the main pool at about 6:00 a.m. to help me make a point. I don't know if you've noticed that each morning, these lounge chairs we're sitting on are draped with towels and other items belonging to passengers who are still back in their staterooms, sound asleep."

"I suppose you're referring to people saving lounge chairs for later use. My friends and I do it all the time."

I guess I should have suspected that Nell was an offender of this timeless and inconsiderate habit people have developed. So I decided that I would pull my prank without her assistance.

"Never mind then," I said. "You're likely to be up a bit later than normal now that you've made friends with

Seamus anyway."

Nelly did not disagree.

The Schism

NOW WE COME to the schism of sorts among cruise-goers. In one camp, you have people who believe they have a right to rise early and reserve their poolside chairs with sundry sunny-day items several hours before they intend to actually sit in them. Some groups or families will designate an early riser to carry an armful of books, sunglasses, or carrying bags to set out on the chairs long before the rest of us even have breakfast. In other cases, it's just a matter of gathering some towels and setting them out on chairs to reserve the required number. This leaves everyone else free to rise as they please, go to breakfast, and then settle into the unofficially reserved chairs.

The other camp (rightfully) thinks this is cheating. They point out that chair-reserving of this nature is against the rules on nearly every cruise ship running today, and for good reason. All those folks who try to secure chairs early are inconveniencing other people on the cruise. The sign at the entrance to the pool states it. The daily bulletin proclaims it. Common sense tells us to abide by it. Yet many guests cannot resist the urge to save lounge chairs around the pool for fear that they won't be available later.

If your ideal cruise involves lounging for most of the day in those absolute-best poolside chairs, I'm sorry to report that these rule-breakers tend to make this a challenging matter. It could be that you will need to get up earlier than you might otherwise wish in exchange for that great chair. This might be the best strategy, after all, as you can always catch up on lost sleep right there in the chair you rose early to secure. Maybe you will get lucky and find a cluster of chairs appropriate for the size of your group in a nice area without even having to cheat and reserve them in advance. People do tend to come and go frequently, as every cruise ship offers plenty of fun activities to compel them to move from time to time. So, sometimes those chairs do come free.

I guess I'm just one of those rare people who likes to wake early, doesn't particularly care where he sits as long as he can read or socialize comfortably, and respects and appreciates all the rules on a cruise ship. Anyway, it seemed to me that a little mischief was in order.

The next morning, just after 6:00 a.m., I visited the pool to find that, as expected, no fewer than two dozen chairs had already been draped with towels. I gathered up the towels, put them in the used-towel basket, and sat down with a cup of coffee. It didn't take long for a man to appear and ask me if I had seen someone remove towels from the chair I was sitting on and the two chairs next to me.

"Good morning," I said, pausing to sip my coffee. "I saw a pool attendant come by a few minutes ago. He must have been cleaning up from last night's activities. Why do you ask?"

"I was saving these chairs for later when my wife and our friends are ready to sit by the pool."

"Is that fair to others who might come and go before you and your friends are ready to visit the pool?"

The look on his face suggested that he thought I should mind my own business. Without hesitation, he proceeded to place four more towels on loungers a bit farther away from where I sat. He grunted as he passed me on the way back to his stateroom for a bit more sleep. As soon as he was out of sight, I did exactly what you might expect.

IF YOU FALL on the wrong side of the schism, I implore you, please, in the future, do me and other guests a favor: follow the rules. Don't save lounge chairs. Sit on them instead.

With that settled, I'll close on a much more positive note. Over the course of that day, as we reached our first port and an exciting day on an island, my wife and I spotted Nell on a number of occasions, always walking hand-in-hand with a man who must have been Seamus. Each time she saw us, she waved and kept walking. I was happy to see her so happy. I could also sense that her mission had very much changed and our time together on this cruise had come to its end.

6
The World's Most Customizable Vacation

LET'S TURN OUR attention to the onboard activities available to you morning, noon, and night, ranging from exertional to sedentary, depending on your mood and motivation. As we did with food and drink, we'll begin in the early morning hours when the fitness center opens and end our discussion with what just might prove to be the highlight of your day, as you're entertained in the theater or one of the many lounges. All told, you can be assured that when your head finally hits the pillow at the end of each night of your cruise, you will sleep soundly and prepare your mind and body for another day full of enjoyment and entertainment.

As the storyteller your humble narrator has shown himself to be, I prefer to relate the onboard activities from the perspective of the people you may meet or at least observe during your cruise. As Nell and Seamus enjoy each other's company, we'll turn our attention to Easygoing Eddie and Energetic Eve, a married couple that my wife and I first stumbled upon in the parking ramp of the cruise terminal prior to the first day of a journey we embarked upon a few years ago.

If, as was the case on this vacation, you are only traveling a short distance to join your ship, you will be able to park your vehicle in a protected garage for the duration of your cruise (for a reasonable fee). As we entered the ramp and pulled into a space, we couldn't help but notice the late-model Cadillac with Florida plates that read "EEANDEE" pulling into the space next to us. Always one to take interest in creative license plates, my curiosity meter spiked. *Surely this means they both have first and last names that start with "E,"* I thought, intent on uncovering the truth.

Mrs. E. was the first to exit the car. As she rushed to open the trunk and grab the luggage, I heard her yell to her husband to get a move on. It seemed she didn't want to be delayed in getting aboard.

In contrast, Mr. E. appeared to be in something less of a hurry. When he finally opened the passenger-side door, he presented as a slightly overweight gentleman adorned in a flower-print shirt, beige shorts, and sneakers that almost perfectly matched the shade of his long, skinny legs that clearly hadn't seen the sun in quite some time.

In my mind, I had already dubbed Mrs. E. "Energetic Eve." She did not wait for her husband to get himself together. Even as he rose to his full height and began stretching outside the car, she was already nearing the elevator.

"Eddie!" she shouted. "I took the heavy one. You grab the other suitcase and get the lead out. I'll meet you at the elevator."

Somewhere deep in my subconscious, I had already known that this man's name would be Eddie, and now he would go by "Easygoing Eddie," whenever and wherever I would see him again. Here was a man clearly more laid back than his wife, a man quite comfortable and used to being in the passenger seat, not only of the car, but of his life. I watched with a half-smile as Eddie managed to follow instructions, grab the second suitcase, and head for the elevator.

"Don't forget to lock the car," he called out.

Immediately there came the telltale *beep-beep* of the Cadillac's doors locking remotely. There the shiny Floridian standard would rest in quiet and shade for the next week.

Meanwhile, the elevator doors nearly closed on Easygoing Eddie as he yanked his rolling luggage in behind him. My wife and I exchanged a smile. Surely, this would be the last we saw of Eve and Eddie on this trip. Given the noise between them, that suited me just fine.

How wrong we were. It never ceases to amaze me how, on every one of the many cruise vacations we have taken—be it with hundreds or even thousands of other guests—certain passengers will keep popping up day in and day out. It gets to the point where I wind up feeling like one of their traveling companions. Long ago, I stopped trying to figure out if this was by pure coincidence or if it had more to do with the amount of time the travelers in question spent in the public venues of the ship. I can only imagine the number of guests who returned home thinking they had gotten to know my dear friend Doug, himself an Energizer Bunny.

In any case, over the course of this cruise, we caught at least a glimpse of Eve and Eddie every day. Sometimes they were together, but more often than not, we spotted them in separate locations. Eddie turned out to be, just as I envisioned, a man who took only the minimum number of steps each day, most of them designed to deliver him to a place where he could sit and relax. We would pass as he lounged by the pool with a book in his hands and earbuds in his ears. We would encounter him on a stool in the sports bar, sipping a beer and watching a college football game. We would witness his snoring from a lounge chair on the leisure deck.

Eve, on the other hand, would rush by on her way to a lecture in the theater, or we would spot her learning the Macarena poolside in the morning. It seems safe to assume that she has never remained seated in one place for more than a few minutes at a time. One evening, we observed Eddie minding a table in the buffet restaurant while Eve secured the food for both of them. Later, Eddie took a nap in the theater before the show as Eve chatted up anyone and everyone within earshot.

As we begin to explore the onboard activities you may avail yourself of on a cruise vacation, I invite you to attach names and faces from your own life to the man climbing the rock wall (clearly not Eddie) or the woman who attempts to cram every single onboard activity into the cruise, quite possibly Eve. You may even choose to add notes or imagined dialogue in the margins of a page when inspiration enters your thoughts.

"Eddie!" your own Eve might shout. "The ballroom dancing class begins in fifteen minutes!"

"Why don't you go and tell me all about it over dinner?" your own Eddie might reply.

"It takes two to do the waltz, the tango, and the cha-cha."

"Maybe you can find a partner once you get there."

Whatever you call your own Eve and Eddie, what makes them such a perfect couple to introduce us to the onboard activities is their willingness to let each other be who they are while allowing the other the space needed to fulfill their own cruise objectives. Obviously, Eddie and Eve had been together for more than a few years and had probably embarked on a number of cruises. How else could such opposing personalities find ways to coexist in the relatively confined setting of a cruise ship?

The bottom line is that no matter what your personality and no matter which cruise you wind up choosing, you are sure to find something to enjoy. You might not bump into Eddie in the yoga class, but that won't deter Eve from stretching every muscle to the soft sound of spa music in the fitness center. While they might spend quite a bit of time apart pursuing their respective interests, the love clearly remains. When your own Eve spots Eddie sitting poolside in the sun, for instance, she will be sure to gently remind him to put a little more lotion on his skin so he doesn't burn. When your own Eddie looks up from his book to notice Eve participating in the belly flop contest, he is sure to smile and cheer.

Speaking of a smiling Eddie, let's start our exploration into onboard activities with something a little more his speed.

Chilling with Easygoing Ed

OUR NEW FRIEND Eddie certainly isn't alone in his cruise-activity preferences. Many people book their cruise vacations with a mind to kick off their shoes and find a comfortable spot aboard the ship to catch up on some reading and writing or just an opportunity to rest and relax. If you're like Eddie, you can be assured that you will have ample time and space for accomplishing your chillout objectives.

On every cruise ship that sails the seas, you will find a number of places to read, write, listen to music, or dive into that audiobook without being interrupted by the more active passengers. First is the balcony of your stateroom (should you book a higher-end cabin, where you can put your feet up on a lounge chair and read while the water flows beneath you). Next, you may venture out to the ship's library and select a book from the inventory of reading materials, be they fiction, non-fiction, or simply a recently published magazine. In the library, you will find comfortable chairs and tables where you can read, write, and enjoy a quiet morning or afternoon. I have spent a reasonable share of time in the library on my current cruise as I write this very book.

Although the various lounges get quite busy in the evening and after dark, throughout the day you will be able to find quiet space in most lounges to accomplish your objectives. If you like to read and enjoy the sunshine at the same time, you will find lounge chairs far enough away from the swimming pool venues to read or write without the usual noise interference.

My wife and I have come to prefer cruises that feature a majority of days at sea with no port visits, in part because we like to avail ourselves of maximum chillout opportunities. On a fourteen-day trip across the ocean, we have been known to awaken early and be the first guests in the fitness center. After an hour of exercise and a quick swim in the pool or a few minutes in the hot tub, we shower, dress, and enjoy a peaceful breakfast at the buffet or in our stateroom.

If we have signed up for a cooking or art class, this will occupy at least a couple of hours to fill out our morning. If we have nothing scheduled, we will sit on our balcony and read one of the several books we have brought with us or have borrowed from the ship's library. Because I read at least three or four books per cruise, I load them onto my iPad to avoid carrying them onboard as added weight to my luggage.

When lunchtime arrives, we usually relax by the pool bar and enjoy our lunch with a glass of beer or wine. In the afternoon, we may choose to watch a movie or even take a short nap. As the afternoon turns toward evening, we may use the liquors we ordered for the room to prepare a cocktail and sit on our balcony while we decide where we want to eat our dinner. Sometimes we take in a lecture in the theater before dinner or enjoy the early stage show after dinner is over. Since we are early risers, it isn't uncommon for us to retire earlier than many of the passengers, unless I feel lucky and venture down to the casino to try my skills at Craps or Blackjack.

While we may repeat some of these activities on an almost daily basis, we try not to pre-plan each day. We will vary our routine regularly enough that it avoids becoming a routine at all. You will be surprised at how quickly time at sea passes, even on a cross-ocean voyage where the ship never enters a port for as many as five or six days in succession.

More Energetic Activities with Eve

IF YOU'RE ANYTHING like Energetic Eve, or for that matter, like my old friend Doug, you will prefer to pack your cruise with wall-to-wall action.

When the ship is on the move at sea, there is no limit to the activities the cruise staff will have scheduled for the enjoyment of those who wish to participate. The only thing to keep in mind on this front is that whenever the ship is in a port of call, shipboard activities will reduce to a minimum, as passengers are encouraged to go ashore and enjoy an excursion or simply step out on their own. The case for this is likely to be even stronger post-COVID, as most ships will want to be as empty as possible while at ports to accommodate vigorous cleaning of the rooms and public spaces.

No matter where you are in the world, the health and fitness center will be open daily, even on port visits, from early in the morning until late into the evening. Passengers may exercise in the fitness center on a variety of machines and other offerings. There is usually a yoga class or organized exercise program several times each day. I am nearly certain that Energetic Eve has yet to miss a class on this cruise.

Continuing with our exercise theme, every ship at sea offers a designated deck for walking or running laps around the perimeter of the vessel. In addition, ships usually have a sports deck with a putting green, basketball and tennis court, and an area to play shuffleboard. Some ships even offer a rock-climbing wall for those more daring passengers.

In the spa, which is adjacent to the fitness center, you may schedule a massage or other body treatment for a fee. Some ships offer a thermal suite and pool with a steam room and sauna. You may also visit the hair salon and enjoy a pedicure or facial treatment while your hair is being done. If they wish, men can schedule a haircut with a shave or a manicure.

Most cruise lines offer religious services that coincide with days of worship for people of all faiths. One cruise company has a tradition of celebrating daily Catholic Mass for those who are interested in attending.

If you like to play parlor games like Trivial Pursuit, jackpot bingo, or games modeled after television gameshows, you are certain to find one or more in which to participate. There will always be an opportunity to join a game of bridge or other card games in a room designated for this purpose.

Poolside during the morning and afternoon hours, you can learn pop-culture-inspired dances like the Macarena, join in a sing-along, or watch the staff race homemade boats in the pool. There will also be ice-sculpting contests, cooking demonstrations, and almost any other activity you can imagine. We have been on cruises that cater to knitting clubs as well, where space is set aside for guests to participate in knitting classes or competitions.

Some cruises invite their guests to become an entertainer for a day by participating in talent shows performed exclusively by passengers. If you think of yourself as the next Susan Boyle, you might try singing "I Dreamed the Dream" before your fellow guests. Believe it or not, some passengers are actually pretty talented.

Taking a chance with lady luck is also an option on most cruise ships. At the onboard casino, you will be able to wager on slot machines or the usual array of table games such as Roulette, Blackjack, Texas Hold 'Em, and Craps. The casino is open when the ship is at sea, from early until the wee hours of the morning, though admittedly the hours on my current cruise have been reduced to account for post-COVID cleaning practices. Whenever the doors are open, they will be happy to either take your money or provide you enough winnings to spend at the next art auction on board. If you have my luck, the former is far more likely.

Speaking of which, throughout your cruise, you may choose to attend an art auction, where skilled professionals expound and display works of art by world-famous artists on which you will be given an opportunity to bid. On the newer or recently renovated ships, you may have the opportunity to make some art of your own as well, either by testing your skills in a cooking class or by joining other artists in the artist loft.

When I have found the energy to stay up late, I have danced the night away in panoramic lounges that turn into dance clubs sometime around midnight. You will likely find Eve there. On more sedentary evenings, we have taken in a first-run movie in a theater created for that purpose. On warm, star-filled nights, we have even enjoyed a movie on the large screen in the pool area of the ship with a bucket of popcorn on our laps. There is where you will find Eddie.

I'm getting a little exhausted by all this activity, so let's return to the sedentary for a while. Throughout the day, you may enjoy attending a presentation by a lecturer who is knowledgeable about specific academic subjects, or even about the port city or culture the ship will be visiting next. On a recent trip to Antarctica, my wife and I learned a great deal of valuable information about how to survive in frigid temperatures at certain times of the year when there are only a couple hours of daylight. We have also attended classes on how best to utilize our electronic devices and the technology that seems to be ever changing.

There will invariably be opportunities to take dance lessons from professional dance instructors, and it is common to see couples learning various forms of ballroom dancing. As evening rolls around, certain lounges will have piano music, a quartet, or even an orchestra playing music. There, you might even be invited to participate on the dance floor.

Whatever activities you prefer, there is never a shortage of things to do, even down to borrowing a board game like Scrabble or chess and taking it to your cabin. As I mentioned previously, if you need some time to curl up privately in your room, you will be able to enjoy a movie of your choice from a large selection available in the library or the offerings on your television.

No matter which activities you favor, they are—at least in your humble narrator's opinion—merely the appetizers for the main course on any cruise: the shows, the live acts, the music, and the incredibly professional entertainment. These offerings are so tremendous that you are sure to find both the Eves and the Eddies of the world seated in eager attendance.

Let Them Entertain You

IN 1959, possibly long before you were old enough to remember or perhaps were even born, a new musical opened on Broadway. Its name was "Gypsy: A Musical Fable," and it starred the voice and talent of the First Lady of Musical Comedy, the late, great Ethel Merman. When Ethel sang, people listened. In this particular musical about Gypsy Rose Lee, she bellowed with her strong mezzo the words to "Let Me Entertain You." This also happens to be the theme of this segment in a chapter dedicated to the tremendous variety of entertainment options one can find on the cruises of the world.

If you are like most cruise guests, when you book your cruise, you will want access to live entertainment, day or night, for every day of your journey. I'm sorry to say that you won't meet Ethel Merman personally, as she died in 1984 at the age of 76. You will meet many extremely talented performers, however, some of whom are beginning their careers and others who have enjoyed their day in the sun already but still know how to capture an audience.

If at any time while waiting for a show or when leaving the theater, you find yourself whistling a happy tune, be certain to give proper credit for the song of that name originally sung by Deborah Kerr in the Broadway musical "The King and I."

Which brings me, in a roundabout way, to Rosemary Clooney. Or at least it brings me to the lady who sang aboard a cruise I enjoyed several years ago for a two-night engagement before she moved on. Likely in her mid-fifties, this wonderful performer bore a startling resemblance to Rosemary Clooney, both in appearance and voice. On the morning after her second show, I happened to spot her having breakfast alone in the buffet. By now, you've gotten to know me, so it won't come as a shock to learn that I couldn't resist approaching and telling her how much I had enjoyed her show. She welcomed me with a smile and asked if I would like to join her.

"It's not every day I receive such a nice compliment," she said as I sat down across from her. "Most passengers are reluctant to approach an entertainer."

"Why's that?"

"Most people assume we want to be left alone and not be bothered."

I shrugged. "I have to admit, I figured that was true too, but I couldn't resist."

"Well, thank you for not resisting. I spend so much time alone that it wears on me after a while. Most of the performers on this ship are half my age. I have far more in common with people in your age group. No offense intended."

Unsure of why that should offend me, I pivoted to asking whether she would be performing again that evening.

"No, unfortunately I'm done on this ship. It's why I'm up so early, actually. I have to leave as soon as we dock."

I was disappointed to learn this news, as it would have been nice to hear her sing again. "Where do you head next?"

"I'm being met at the dock to catch a flight to a different ship, where I'll perform for two nights before moving on again."

"Tough schedule."

"In this business, you tend to live out of a suitcase. But if you want to continue performing, you get used to it."

"Must be difficult bouncing from place to place."

"Difficult? Maybe. At my age, I take every call I can from my agent. For every one of me, there are a hundred others who would jump at the chance to sing before a live audience."

The idea of having to do all this to hang on to the spotlight fascinated me, so I asked how she'd gotten her start in show business.

"I was barely twenty. I happened to be singing in a small lounge on the Vegas strip when none other than Frank Sinatra passed by on his way through the hotel. He stopped for a minute to hear me sing. Within two weeks, I was singing as the opening act for his main performance. He must have liked what he heard."

"Sinatra," I said, flabbergasted. "That's the break of a lifetime."

She explained how Sinatra moved on from her after a couple of years, but the doors had been opened wide and she was able to capitalize. At the risk of seeming rude, I couldn't resist asking if performing on a cruise ship was a letdown for a woman of her talent.

She shook her head. "I'll keep accepting gigs for as long as my phone rings and my voice holds up." Then she shook my hand. "I want to thank you for stopping by. Your kind words have made my day."

At that moment, the ship's horn announced our arrival at the dock. "I wish you a safe journey," I said. "I hope you're as well received on your next ship as you were here. I feel certain you will be."

She thanked me again, stood, and gave me a friendly hug before we went our separate ways. I hope her phone rings off the hook for many years to come.

My new friend's story, while intriguing, is certainly not unique. As she mentioned, she is just one of many performers who live this lifestyle. I can only imagine the lives of the entertainers who come aboard for short stays and those who live on the ship as part of the main troupe of performers employed by the cruise company. Stories of success and of heartbreak must abound. For the purposes of this book, however, we'll focus instead on the more observable side of their craft.

The first night of your cruise will be an eye-opener, to say the least. In the main theater, you will likely be given your first taste of what to expect from the permanent cast aboard the ship. Their production will offer the chance to judge not only their talent level but also the genre of material you may expect throughout the voyage. If you are sailing with passengers mostly up in years, you may see more of the kind of entertainment I referenced at the start of this chapter. If you are part of a mix of young and not-so-young passengers, the material will attempt to strike an appropriate balance more suited to what you are likely to enjoy. Meanwhile, family friendly ships will offer family-oriented shows with something to please all age groups.

Whatever kind of cruise you book, don't be concerned about whether the material will suit the audience, as this is not the cruise company's first rodeo. They're well aware of the demographics of their passengers. The other piece you can count on is that your cruise's entertainer cast will include an orchestra, always composed of extremely talented musicians who adapt well to the differing forms of entertainment they support.

Before or after the show in the main theater, provided you're willing to wander around a little, you'll also get a feel for the shows on hand in the various lounges. You may find your attention drawn to the talents of a pianist. Further along, you might hear the sound of laughter as a top-notch comedian plies his or her trade. If you enjoy jazz, you may soon find yourself seated in a lounge listening to a band in full swing.

The entertainment will vary from evening to evening, but the main cast members generally perform three or four nights each week, and there is always a new show on stage for you to enjoy. On the other nights, guest performers will arrive, just like the singer I met over breakfast. At the start of your cruise, perhaps the cast will stage a musical or play. The next night, the main performer might be a magician. The next evening could be a musician, then a singer, and perhaps a comedian. These acts will be of high enough caliber to warrant their welcome to the stage in the main theater. You might be familiar with some of the entertainers' names, while others will be working their way up the ladder in the industry.

Depending on where in the world your cruise is sailing, entertainment may come aboard for part of a day or evening to introduce you to the music and dance unique to that locale. You may have an opportunity to watch Irish tap dancers from Dublin, Flamenco dancers from Buenos Aires, or Russian acrobats from St. Petersburg. On occasion, school children will arrive in traditional dress and win your heart with a song or two they have learned especially for you.

There will also be opportunities to leave the vessel and enjoy a concert, play, or opera performed in that particular port of call. My wife and I have been fortunate to hear the Vienna Boys Choir in person, attend an open-air opera in Paris, take in a circus in Budapest, tour a school in Mexico, and listen to a native Alaskan tell the history of her region while overlooking Mt. McKinley in Denali.

Toward the end of your cruise, your crew will put on a show of their own in the main theater. Many guests attend as a way of saying thank you for the service they have received. The theater will be filled to capacity. I believe you will enjoy what the crew has produced for your pleasure.

There is so much more I could write about entertainment possibilities during your cruise, but I believe you have a fair picture of what to expect. Have fun, and enjoy what there is to enjoy.

7
Stepping Out

HERE MY WIFE and I have come to the first port of call on this extraordinary cruise. You will find on your own cruise that some guests like to take full advantage of the change of scenery offered at each port. They will rise early to debark and enjoy the local food, drinks, culture, and adventurous excursions as soon as possible. Others will take their time going ashore, whether because they haven't planned an excursion, they're having too much fun on the ship itself, or they prefer the Easygoing Eddie chillout approach.

No matter what kind of cruise-goer you are, I highly encourage you to step out and explore your first port of call, especially if this is your first-ever cruise vacation. If nothing else, it's nice to stretch your legs and work off a few of the calories the buffet has helped you store in your body.

Guests cruise for many different reasons, but high on the list of priorities is the chance to visit interesting venues in the region of the world in which the cruise sails. Unless you are sailing on one of those ocean-crossing cruises where the ship may not dock for as many as five or six successive days, your vessel is likely to arrive in a different port four or five times each week. Post-COVID, it is likely that these port stops will be reduced to two or three, with each stop featuring more than one day's opportunity to go ashore. Either way, the port calls afford passengers an opportunity to see the sights special to that locale.

As your cruise pulls up alongside the dock, take a look over the side of the ship and you will notice a large number of buses, vans, and taxi cabs lined up waiting for guests to exit the vessel. In a short period of time, those vehicles will be filled with a large majority of your fellow cruise passengers eager to explore what the port has to offer.

If you are among those who have decided to go ashore, plenty of excitement awaits you. Depending on the weather, the amount of time your ship will be in port, and the research you have done before leaving home, you may be dressed in a bathing suit, walking attire, or even bundled up in cold weather clothing as you leave your stateroom and head for the gangway.

This is, of course, an exciting thought. But let's not get ahead of ourselves. For now, keep in mind that the question of whether or not to book an excursion is one of the more challenging choices you will face on any cruise—even more challenging than deciding in which restaurant to enjoy your next meal or pre-dinner cocktail. The variety of cruise-sponsored excursions will be considerable enough on its own to give some cruise-goers a sense of vertigo. That's even before you consider the option of choosing an independent tour for yourself and/or your group. Let's face it. Some of us have planning-related limitations that others do not. Some are totally self-sufficient when it comes to planning and executing. Others are more content to have professionals guide them from place to place. Much also will depend on where you are visiting on any given day.

This chapter will help you navigate your excursions, whether you go with the cruise-sponsored variety or venture off on your own.

Letting the Cruise Line Do the Work

MANY PASSENGERS WHO go ashore will have purchased an excursion package from the cruise line. Depending on the port, the cruise will offer as many as a dozen different excursions to choose from. Some will consume your entire day, while others will last only for several hours. These excursions are extremely nice in the sense that they bring plenty of action and variability to your cruise, and also because they are cruise-line sponsored and therefore take all planning out of your hands.

In deciding whether to book a cruise-line-sponsored tour and which one to book, be sure to spend some time reading the information the cruise line has prepared to assist you in making your selection. In great detail, they will advise you what you will see on each excursion, how long you will be on the tour, and the level of endurance the tour will require.

The form will also advise you of the cost of the tour. Although you may be shocked at the price, please realize that the cruise line will have to pay for buses, their drivers, guides, and entry fees to venues. Perhaps you have booked a cruise that includes unlimited excursions as part of the cost, in which case you will be pleased that your credit card won't wind up over its limit at the end of your voyage (assuming it wasn't there already when you started.).

If you have opted to join one of the many exciting excursions, you will be directed to a meeting place aboard the ship at an appointed hour after the ship docks. There, you will gather with the other passengers joining you on the same excursion. With the lessons of the pandemic in mind, these gatherings are unlikely to be as heavily populated as they used to be. Now, a larger number of excursions depart at staggered intervals to allow for less densely packed buses and social distancing. Either way, don't be late, as excursions have been known to leave without the full load of passengers.

Some people find cruise-line-sponsored excursions somewhat restricting, as you are beholden to the plan the cruise company puts together. Others find them invigorating, exciting, and uniquely positioned to introduce the local culture. Whichever camp you fall into, any excursion you partake in is likely to become one of your favorite and most enduring memories of the vacation.

On any given cruise, my wife and I will determine which days and ports will be better for joining a cruise-line-sponsored excursion rather than venturing out on our own or simply staying aboard to enjoy our ship. Our decision is usually based on several factors:

Will there be a language barrier?

This piece can vary in priority based on how skillful you are with languages. In any case where the local culture speaks a language that my wife and I share fluently, we will happily venture out on our own. If we are unfamiliar with the language and have reason to believe that navigating the culture without a translator will be challenging, we are more likely to opt for a cruise-line-sponsored tour, as they always come with guides who can help us communicate.

Are we in a country that has strict rules that visitors must follow?

Your cruise provider will share these rules with you prior to any stop at a port of call, but they vary drastically depending on where in the world you find yourself. Caribbean islands tend to be comparatively lax on the rules front, but places like Russia, China, and much of Southeast Asia will present with more rigorous rule sets.

In any situation where the rules are more restrictive, it might be safer (and it is almost always easier) to venture out on a cruise-led excursion rather than going it alone.

How far away from the ship will this excursion travel? And how many different places will the tour take us?

The time and energy that goes into each excursion varies, so it is important to take the rigor into consideration. There is always a delicate balance between time, energy, and the quality of the sights and experiences you will enjoy on the excursion in question.

It really is a matter of weighing the pros and cons of any tour. When we have visited China and Russia, countries with so much to see yet so many rules to follow, we have always opted to join a cruise-line-sponsored tour. We have never been unsatisfied with this decision. For instance, I can't imagine touring the Hermitage Museum and both Catherine's and Peter's palaces in St. Petersburg on the same day without the help of our English-speaking guide and a knowledgeable driver to get us there and back. The same would be true of navigating the streets of Shanghai or Beijing, cities we came halfway around the world to enjoy and explore.

We also have joined excursions in ports on Caribbean islands simply because of the compelling nature of the planned itinerary. On one such adventure, we visited a sugar plantation, enjoyed a tropical lunch served in a tiki hut, and were afforded some time to swim in the turquoise waters off a white-sand beach at a location we would never have found on our own.

While my wife and I are not likely to participate in more than a few cruise-line-sponsored excursions on any given voyage, we certainly can understand why some passengers sign up for as many excursions as possible. Some even do more than one on a given day, if time permits.

Other times, you just don't have a choice. Cruise-sponsored excursions have proven to be a necessity in certain ports, if for no other reason than it is the only possible way to see what there is to be seen. How many of us can find and explore a rainforest without a guide to show us the way? Are you willing to venture sixty miles inland to visit a shrine or famous temple and not be concerned about returning to the ship before it leaves port? If so, you're more adventurous than I, which is admirable—just don't be late in returning to the ship or the nature of your vacation will change drastically.

Whatever you decide regarding excursions, I can't stress enough that the really good ones will be among the most memorable parts of any trip. In all the years and on all the cruises we have taken, one of my all-time favorite memories is of a cruise-line-sponsored excursion on Christmas Day in Vienna, Austria. The experience came right in the middle of a Danube River cruise. We left the ship with our guide early in the morning and took in the sights of beautiful Vienna, both from our bus and on foot. At 11:00 a.m., we left the tour to attend Christmas Mass at the Cathedral, where we were treated to organ music and a concert sung by the Vienna Boys Choir.

After Mass, we rejoined the tour and visited Schönbrunn Palace and a Christmas market. We returned to the ship for a turkey dinner with all the trimmings before venturing out once more to attend a concert featuring the music of Mozart, Bach, and Beethoven. When our day ended, my wife and I looked at each other and realized that this had been a special Christmas indeed. Had we elected to experience Vienna on our own, we may have enjoyed some of these adventures, but surely not all of them, and certainly not in the well-planned, carefree manner in which we did. There really is something to be said for letting the cruise line do the work from time to time.

On Your Way, On Your Own

OF COURSE YOU don't always have to leave matters in the hands of the cruise line. Many vacationers enjoy venturing into a port city or locale on their own. Sometimes, they do this because they prefer the freedom, the lack of strict scheduling, the relative unpredictability, and the chance to see a location independently rather than alongside their fellow cruise-goers. Other times, they aren't inspired by the array of excursions offered by the cruise line and would rather make their own fun. Still other times, they wish to see the culture firsthand and meet the locals in ways and settings that aren't always available on the cruise-line-sponsored tours.

If you have arranged your own independent tour with friends, you will head for the gangway, where you will meet your tour guide and begin your day. If, on the other hand, you have decided to tour alone or as a couple, you may choose to wait for the crowd to thin out and venture ashore a bit later. There, you might engage a taxi driver or simply walk to town or a nearby beach.

The best advice if you have decided to strike out on your own is to make a plan and follow it. Be certain to leave enough time to get back aboard before the horn blows, signifying that the ship is leaving the dock. Before you go anywhere, pick up your phone and program in the numbers that will allow you to contact the ship and also the local police in the event something doesn't go according to plan. Your cruise will have these numbers on hand. Ask any member of the staff, and they will help you find them.

The next piece of advice is to know as much as possible about where you are heading and who is taking you there and back. Carry as little cash as possible, and please do not be walking in tight alleyways, especially after dark. You should also keep a copy of your passport and an acceptable credit card in your pocket—somewhere separate from your wallet or handbag, in case one of them is lost or stolen. Now, when I write this, please note that I am in no way attempting to dissuade you from venturing out on your own. I am simply encouraging you to bring your common sense along with you.

Many of the best days my wife and I have spent ashore have been on our own, either on foot or by taxi. If this sounds appealing, do keep in mind that a walk through the streets of Paris may well differ from a walk through the bazaar in Istanbul. It is always better to be well informed of the local culture and well prepared in the event that something goes wrong.

On days when my wife and I have chosen not to join a cruise-line-sponsored tour and instead explore a port of call on our own, we have been fortunate to experience things and meet people that would not have been possible if we had taken a formal tour.

Take, for instance, our day in Dubrovnik, Croatia, when we enjoyed a leisurely breakfast in the nearly empty buffet and waited for the tour participants to debark. It was late morning when we walked down the gangway and spotted a young man standing by his car with a nice smile on his face. He approached and asked us in perfect English if we would allow him to show us his city. We immediately agreed, and off we went to see the sights.

"My name is Josip," our guide said. "This is Croatian for 'Joseph.'"

We introduced ourselves and then sat back while Josip enchanted us with his vast knowledge of his birth city. It did not take long for us to recognize that we had made a wise decision in accompanying him.

After touring for an hour, Josip asked if we would like to meet his mother and enjoy lunch in his family home. Now, how often does something like this occur? At the same time, Josip was a stranger to us, so I took a moment to think about whether to accept.

The quick affirmative reply from my wife let me know that we would be heading next to Josip's childhood home. Any effort to tell you just how special a day this proved to be would not do it justice. This is simply something you have to experience firsthand.

That evening, with our time of departure still several hours out, Josip drove us to a restaurant overlooking the Adriatic Sea and encouraged us to have a leisurely dinner while he attended to some chores. We agreed to have him pick us up in two hours to return us to the ship. Off he went.

As we sat outdoors under the stars and looked out to sea, we were treated to a wonderful meal and a terrific bottle of wine. Dubrovnik, because of Josip, has risen high on my list of favorite places we have visited.

On another trip several years ago, I sailed unaccompanied across the Atlantic for sixteen days—a wonderful experience I will never forget. I got to spend some time alone, reading and writing, taking meals in my cabin, and if I snored, there was no one there to hear me. I slept like a baby. Anyway, that is beside the point. When the ship arrived in the Mediterranean, I chose to go ashore in Florence, Rome, and Monte Carlo. To get from the port to visit Rome, one takes a train ride of approximately an hour. On the train, I met a family from South America, who graciously invited me to dine with them when we returned to the ship. It was both fun and informative to meet them and learn more about their culture. Later, when we docked in Florence, a Vietnamese couple sat with me on the train and asked if I would help them navigate the city, as they learned I was generally familiar with what to explore in a limited amount of time. I served in the U.S. Army during the Vietnam War, and although I was spared overseas duty, I learned more about that war and Vietnamese culture in the ten hours we were together than I had learned in the forty-plus years since the conflict ended.

Now, these memories I hold in high regard for obvious reasons. There are other memories I could share that stand out because we (read "I") didn't plan thoroughly enough and didn't get quite so lucky.

A long, long time ago, we docked in Budapest, Hungary, for two days. On the evening of the first day, my wife and I decided to dine at Gundel, a world-famous restaurant that dates to the 1850s. Gundel is located across the river in Pest, which before it merged in the late 1800s with Buda—thus becoming Budapest—was a city unto itself. Being a bit stubborn, I convinced my wife that we could manage this trip by using public transportation. It was only after boarding the bus in Buda to cross the river to Pest that I realized we were lost with no one to show us directions, as English was not widely spoken in Budapest at the time.

Fortunately for us, a young man named Gabor was riding the bus. He spoke fluent English and offered to guide us to the restaurant and then meet us after dinner to assist in our return to our ship. After dinner, we asked

Gabor what he was doing for the next day and a half.

"I am starting a new job," he said, "but that does not begin until next week. So I am free."

We learned that Gabor had access to a motor vehicle, and so we made arrangements to hire him as our tour guide for the remainder of our time in Budapest. I will always remember the next day, when he picked us up early in the morning and stayed with us until dark. He showed us both cities and taught us the history of his country, including the innumerable times Hungary had been invaded by its Turkish neighbors. When we visited the Museum of History, Gabor explained the importance of each piece of art.

At the end of our time with Gabor, as we were paying him for his services, he asked for one small favor.

"Of course," I said.

"When you return home," he said, "if you could find a set of dog tags on a silver chain—similar to the ones American GIs wear—and you could have my name engraved on them and sent to me, I would be grateful."

We took down Gabor's address and promised that we would try. Fortunately, we were able to honor his request. We kept in touch with Gabor for many years thereafter.

Of course, there are other ways to go it alone without simply wandering onto the dock and looking for a local tour guide. You can also call ahead to your port cities and arrange more official private tours from companies unaffiliated with your cruise line. We have done this often. One of the best experiences happened near the end of a twenty-day cruise from Santiago, Chile, to Antarctica and then the Falkland Islands before completing our voyage in Buenos Aires, Argentina.

In the final city, we had approximately ten hours to spend before we would be flying home, so we contacted a company called Tours by Locals and arranged a private tour of Buenos Aires and its environs.

We were greeted by a lovely young lady named Sofia, who had been born and raised in this beautiful area of South America. In our time together, we learned much of the history of this country and city and were fortunate to visit the grave of Eva Maria Duarte de Peron, the First Lady of Argentina from 1946 until her untimely death from cancer in 1952 at the young age of 33. Whenever I think of this experience, I can hear in my head the beautiful song "Don't Cry For Me Argentina" from the musical *Evita,* which details the life of Eva Peron.

This tour serves as a reminder to us that when given the opportunity to visit a country or city along our voyage, we may have the option of booking a tour that will offer us the ability to do and see things that we have researched before leaving home to join our cruise. We have availed ourselves of this alternative in any number of destinations we have been fortunate to visit over our many years of cruising.

Oh, the People You'll Meet

ON ANY EXCURSION—particularly those sponsored by the cruise line—you are likely to meet any number of charming characters (although keep in mind that "charming" is a relative term). I remember well an excursion my wife and I took that put us in the company of a man so much like the character of Archie Bunker from the long-running television series "All in the Family" that we might as well just call him Archie. I mean this not in the sense that he used similarly offensive language or perspectives on American culture, but in the sense that he was no stranger to shouting, to a general reticence to leave his chair, or to having a beer in his hand at all times.

We first met Archie as we exited our ship to participate in a shore excursion to a seventeenth-century castle in Scotland, a visit preceded by a rather long bus ride to a restored village in the region. On the gangway, we found the queue (not a "line," since we were in the United Kingdom) already forming, passengers standing in far closer quarters than they have been in this post-COVID world. Through the crowd boomed a male voice.

"How did I let you get me into this?"

"Oh, honey," came the soft reply of an impossibly patient woman. "Give it a chance. Let's just have a nice day together."

"A nice day is watching football in the sports bar with a beer in my hand."

While I can't condone Archie's tone or tenor, he did have a point. Because so many people choose to book excursions or take advantage of the tours on offer, some people prefer to spend port days on the ship to take advantage of its relative emptiness.

"Why don't you go ahead?" Archie said gruffly. "I'll still be here when you return, and you'll know where to find me."

I have to admit that right at that moment, I could relate to Archie's hesitance. As informative and fun as a tour might be, there are certain drawbacks, like sitting on a bus for hours with people you don't know. Occasionally, one of those people can be a grouch like Archie.

"I promise we'll have fun," his wife said. "And after I shop for a few minutes, we can grab a beer in one of those old Scottish pubs."

"Are you serious? The shops will be full of stuff we don't need and the beer at the pubs is probably watered down."

The queue began to move. All at once, we were boarding our bus. You can guess who wound up choosing a seat right behind us (hey, that's at least one advantage of the post-COVID bus restrictions: you can be sure that no Archies sit immediately behind you anymore).

"Where's the bus driver?" Archie started barking a few minutes after he sat down. "The other buses left ten minutes ago, and we boarded before them. Who's running this show anyway?"

Fortunately for all of us, the driver arrived soon after, and we pulled away from the dock.

"Who taught this guy how to drive?" Archie said, loudly enough for the driver to hear. "He's on the wrong side of the road."

"Honey?" his poor wife said. "Don't you remember? They drive on the opposite side over here."

If you think that shut him up, you would be mistaken.

"I'm having trouble hearing the guide. You should have gotten us seats in the front of the bus."

Thank goodness we arrived at the village in a shorter time than expected. As we were leaving the bus, we gave Archie and his wife a wide berth and set off on our own to explore.

Part two of the bus ride proved a little more subdued, as Archie seemed pleased with the statue of Queen Elizabeth he had purchased and the Union Jack shirt he was now wearing. At first, I figured he must have changed shirts in the dressing room, but then I pictured him just tearing off his shirt and putting on the new one in broad view of the whole shop, and that vision somehow made more sense.

"I sure hope this driver knows where he's going," Archie announced to no one in particular. "I don't want to get lost and be stuck here with these guys who wear skirts instead of pants. No wonder they needed us to win the war."

As an aside, Edinburgh Castle, not unlike most of the historically significant places we have been able to enjoy on other tour excursions, was worth every minute and penny we spent on the six-hour visit. We would do it again in a heartbeat. In fact, we plan to do it again next year.

The trip back to the ship was comparatively peaceful. Archie only complained for a minute, gave his wife a back-handed compliment, and then fell asleep.

Just before he passed out, he said, "I don't know if you had much to do with this tour, but I must admit it was pretty enjoyable. The beer was better than I thought, even if the glass wasn't filled to the top, and I'm sure you can wash my new shirt tonight in the sink so I can wear it again tomorrow."

Thankfully, Archie slept the rest of the way back. Other than his snoring, the only sounds we heard were the sighs coming from his wife.

Of course by sharing this story, I don't mean to discourage you from taking excursions. For every Archie, there are a hundred or more passengers who never complain and who enjoy every minute of the tour as much as you will enjoy it. People can sometimes be abrasive, but a little headache is often worth it for the chance to see Buckingham Palace in London, fly over a glacier in

Alaska, visit the beaches of Normandy, experience the vineyards of Bordeaux, or stand in awe of the Opera House in Sydney.

Having an experienced guide to take you through these memorable sights leads to a great deal more insight and information. Also, knowing that the tour is cruise-line sponsored helps relieve the stress of travel, as you will always know where you need to be, when you need to be there, and how you will get from one place to another. A truculent fellow traveler is usually a small price to pay for not having to arrange transportation, navigate language barriers, purchase tickets, and stand in line for an hour or more waiting to gain entry to an attraction.

Customs and Risks

ONE OF THE best parts about going ashore at port is the people-watching. I'll have more to say on the subject of my favorite pastime in a later chapter, but for now, a word of warning: if you're a people-watcher like me, one of the people you should be watching is yourself.

On a visit to a coastal port in Spain, I was approached by a woman wearing a nun's habit. She was holding a young boy by the hand.

"Mister," she said, "would you give a small donation to help the poor?"

As I reached into my pocket, the boy stepped forward and hugged me around the waist. This was unexpected enough, but then I felt his hand in my pocket, clenching around my wallet. I jolted, he withdrew, and he and the would-be sister-of-the-poor took off with lightning speed. These days, no matter where in the world we find ourselves, I scrutinize the nuns more closely to see if they're wearing laced-up sneakers under their habits.

Pickpockets are prevalent in many parts of the world, and travelers would be wise to carry important papers and money at or near important parts of their bodies. Women should snuggle their handbags close and men should make use of the front pocket of their pants, as it's harder for thieves to steal from this location.

You might be inclined to believe that the higher the poverty rate in a given country, the higher the potential to run into pickpockets, but that isn't necessarily true. Pickpockets are present in wealthy nations just as well. Meanwhile, some of the poorest people you encounter would never think to make you or anyone else a victim.

Another cultural consideration that may or may not be in your travel guide or the rules shared with you by the cruise line relates to taking photographs. If you happen upon any locals whose picture you would like to take, be polite and ask permission first. Some cultures consider photo-taking rude, particularly if you're trying to capture the essence of how a local person lives, what they eat, what craft they have mastered, and so on. Some tourist locations forbid picture-taking as well. Others allow picture-taking while outlawing the infamous selfie. As a rule—and this applies to so much more than just taking pictures—be polite and respectful of the people around you, and you will be fine.

Wherever you dock, you should also spend some time thinking about what you will wear to shore. Different cultures have wildly different standards of dress from what you might be used to. Sometimes it's more obvious, such as cultures that require women to wear headscarves. In other locations, it is less so.

Once, on a stop in Monaco, the first thing I noticed was the array of private yachts docked in the harbor, some so large and magnificent that they looked startlingly similar to the cruise ship we were deboarding. As we headed toward the gangway alongside our fellow cruise-goers, we couldn't help standing out because of our attire. Most everyone else wore shorts, shirts, and walking shoes. I wore a sport coat packed specifically for this occasion, along with a nice pair of slacks and a button-down shirt. My wife wore a lovely summer-weight dress and shoes with low heels.

"Are you meeting the prince and his wife for lunch?" someone asked with a smirk.

"I bet you a buck they have a limousine waiting for them," I overheard another passenger say.

"No, we're just walking up the hill to have lunch at the Cafe du Paris. They require gentlemen to wear a sport coat and women to wear dresses. After lunch, we'll cross the street and try our luck in the Monte Carlo Casino."

This seemed to appease the people we were talking to, though I noticed that several others in the crowd suddenly looked anxious, as if they hadn't considered the possibility of a dress code at any of the local stops.

While we're on the subject of casinos, I should return to the subject of grift. Pickpockets aren't the only would-be criminals to keep an eye out for in the various ports. For our story, let's stick with Monte Carlo, where the casino is as opulent as every other place in that shockingly wealthy city. On our visit, I immediately headed for the dice table, where at two in the afternoon, I was lucky to find a spot to join the action. At Monte Carlo, there are two casino floors from which to play games of chance, the upper floor being reserved for invited guests. As you may have guessed, we were not among the invited that day, fancy dress or otherwise.

We weren't in the casino for more than a short while before I noticed a man wearing a tuxedo with his tie undone. This man stood at the other end of the table, and he was betting heavily. He looked just like Omar Sharif, the actor who costarred with Julie Christie in the classic film "Dr. Zhivago."

"Omar Sharif," I whispered to my wife.

"Spot on!" she said.

As time passed, Omar appeared to be losing quite a significant sum. I was modestly in the black somehow. Soon, I felt a tap on my shoulder and was surprised to see the Sharif lookalike.

"My name is Peter Forester," he said. "I wonder if I might buy you and your wife a cocktail."

We introduced ourselves, then ordered some drinks as Peter shared the story of how he had come to Monaco to hide from his soon-to-be ex-wife.

"My mother bequeathed me a generous inheritance," Peter explained. "And my ex is doing everything in her power to cash in on it."

As intriguing as this story promised to be, I was more interested in why he had singled the two of us out for drinks.

"I like Americans more than I like the French who pack this casino every night," he said with a shrug.

We accepted this explanation and got back to making small talk. Things were going along nicely until Peter turned the subject to money.

"I am soon to be worth millions in your currency," he said. "But until my divorce is finalized, I sometimes find myself a bit short on cash. I noticed you were winning, so I thought maybe you could stake me a few hundred to get back in the action."

Out of the corner of my eye, I noticed that my wife's jaw had dropped just as far as my own.

"It's interesting to learn that you and I are in the same boat," I said to Peter, thinking about our escape quickly. "You see, the lovely lady sitting here between us is not my wife. She is—how do I put this?—the other woman. Like you, I'm going through a divorce, and I'm playing dice with the few hundred bucks my friend gave to me because she feels sorry for me. So I'm sorry to inform you that you've picked the wrong mark."

My wife and I rose to leave.

"Now if you'll excuse us," I said with a note of finality, "we're heading out to see the sights. Thanks for the drink."

We exited the casino grinning from ear to ear, our jaws fully recovered and back in the proper place.

Opposite Direction

WHETHER YOU WANT to avoid your fellow cruise-goers or the locals hoping to take advantage of the tourists, or if you just want to encounter something that few travelers get to experience, there is wisdom in considering the direction that everyone is heading, and then plotting a route that will take you in the opposite direction. No matter where you are, there can be rewards for going against the grain.

For instance, while docked in Civitavecchia, the port in the Mediterranean that accesses Rome, my wife and I excitedly embarked on a plan to spend a very full day sightseeing. Eager as we were, we exited the ship just as soon as passengers were cleared to disembark. We knew the drill and wasted little time making our way to the train station, a short ten-minute walk from the dock. There, we would catch the train that travels from the port to the city. Many of our fellow passengers followed the same path to this point, but soon we would go our separate ways. There is, after all, much to see and do in Rome. We knew from experience that there would be lines forming early in the day to enter the major venues. We just hoped that the order we chose would minimize the time spent in line.

For today's activities, we had preordered tickets to visit the Sistine Chapel and hoped to spend as much time as possible in the presence of Michelangelo's greatest accomplishment. On a previous visit, because we hadn't preordered tickets, we had waited well over an hour to enter the chapel. Then, once inside, we were moved along by the staff at a rapid pace to allow for the many visitors who would arrive after us.

Upon our arrival at the entrance on this particular day, we were pleased to notice that the line was almost nonexistent. We were ushered into the chapel immediately, where we were thrilled to find that no one was urging us to move along. Because we had elected to get such an early start to the day, we were able to stand stationary for as long as we wished, viewing the vaulted ceiling and the wonderful works of art depicting the life of Christ and the history of the world God had created, as seen through the eyes and the brush strokes of the master Michelangelo.

It wasn't until we exited the chapel and headed in the direction of St. Peter's Square that we began to see the mass of people walking toward us. All at once, we realized the other reason we had been able to enjoy such an unfettered look at the chapel: Pope John Paul II had been holding an audience for the assembled masses in the square at the same time.

Yes, our early start had helped, but as fate would have it, we had done something that qualified as "opposite direction" from a large number of people visiting the Eternal City that morning. While everyone was taking in the Pope's words, we were looking at the most famous ceiling in the world. Then, while everyone was herding toward the chapel, we were heading in the opposite direction to see the square. As it happened, we also had the good fortune to see the Pope shortly before his departure from the square. We patted ourselves on the back for having been so lucky.

"Opposite direction" opportunities may happen, whether by pure luck or by accident, but if you plan carefully, you can make them happen just as well. Take, for instance, the likelihood that most of your fellow cruise-goers will be lining up to exit the ship at a port of call as soon as the ship has arrived. Maybe in your opinion this port isn't going to be as busy or exciting as, let's say, Barcelona or Venice. In your view, this is a port city you could explore in maybe half the time that the ship will be docked. What's the rush to disembark after standing in line for forty-five minutes, when you will have your pick of a table where you can enjoy a leisurely breakfast before making your way into town?

Although this rarely happens, weather conditions may also cause a change to your itinerary. For us, it was October, 2012. We were scheduled to attend a wedding not far from Baltimore, Maryland. As we planned our trip to the wedding, I convinced my wife that we should enjoy a seven-day cruise to Bermuda and back from the Port of Baltimore the week before the ceremony.

We arrived in Baltimore on a beautiful fall day, and although the news was reporting the growing strength of Hurricane Sandy off the coast of Cuba, we shrugged, thinking it wouldn't affect our cruise.

Upon checking out of our hotel and heading to the port, we learned that Hurricane Sandy was expected to hug the east coast of the United States for the next several days. Were we not on the east coast of the United States about to enter the Atlantic Ocean on our way to Bermuda? Oh well. We were already in Baltimore, and we knew that the captain and crew would be well advised of the weather conditions and the forecast for the upcoming days.

On our arrival at the port, the storm had become a genuine threat, so we were moderately surprised to find that the ship was boarding passengers. The captain must have known something we didn't know. Why else would we be boarding?

The ship was set to sail at 5:00 p.m., so when 6:00 p.m. and 7:00 p.m. came and went and we were still moored to the dock, we assumed that we would learn about the cancellation of our trip at any moment.

To our surprise, we were instead given an option.

"Because of the impending storm," the cruise director announced, "it might be difficult to actually land in Bermuda."

So they gave an option to the 1,800 passengers aboard. We could either leave the ship and receive a refund and future cruise credits or we could stay aboard and wait out the storm with an additional $800 of ship-board credit.

After the announcement, people started moving about, not just in opposite directions, but in all directions. As many passengers quickly decided to abandon ship, gather their belongings, and head for safer places, others, some on their third or fourth cocktail, were having difficulty making a decision about anything at all.

My wife and I are moderately adventurous, but the controlling decision for us was more geared to what we would do for the next week, since we had to be in Baltimore in a week's time for the wedding.

We decided to stay on board. For the next two hours, we watched approximately half of the passengers prepare to leave the ship. The conversations we overheard are themselves worthy of a chapter, but they will remain unwritten. Suffice to say, in certain couples, certain people are clearly in charge while certain others are not. We were privy to more than a few heated exchanges between couples who couldn't agree. We also learned that $800 of onboard credit can make sailors out of otherwise timid souls.

At 11:00 p.m., the ship's horn announced that the vessel was off its moorings. Given that so many people had decided not to stay on this cruise, our ship was half as heavy as it had been just a short while earlier, and that made a huge and immediately apparent difference on the choppy sea.

There stood my wife and me on our balcony, just hoping we had made a wise decision. Then, as we headed east toward Bermuda, the sky full of beautiful stars, I dismissed the idea that a hurricane could possibly ruin the week. But somewhere out there in the darkness, creeping up on us from our starboard side, was Hurricane Sandy.

After a fitful night's sleep, we awoke early to a rolling sea. We were well out into the Atlantic by then, but still comfortable with our decision to stay aboard. As the day progressed and we enjoyed a beverage—on the house, since $800 goes a long way to ensuring happiness—the seas began to stir to the point where it was difficult to tell whether we owed the swaying sensation to the sea or the free cocktails.

The captain came over the PA system that night to advise us that a landing in Bermuda definitely would not be happening.

"We're going to have to head back toward the east coast and find a safe place to wait out the storm," he explained.

Heavy seas greeted us the next morning, but so did an overabundant breakfast at the buffet. The swaying had gotten so considerable that exercise on the treadmill was out of the question. Skipping this part of the routine did not exactly bother me.

By nightfall, the captain had obtained permission to enter Chesapeake Bay and locate a safe place to drop anchor. This proved especially reassuring, since the hurricane was fast approaching. We decided to dine in a specialty restaurant and use some of our credit on food instead of alcohol.

The morning of our third day was a time we will remember and cherish forever. We stepped out onto our balcony to be greeted by a fleet of United States Navy ships that had left port because of the storm and were anchored with us in the middle of the bay. That day, we learned that ships fare better at sea than they do at the dock, as it is hard to damage a ship with water but quite easy to destroy a vessel if it is attached to land. Needless to say, it was reassuring to know we were as close to protective custody as one could be at a time of such uncertainty.

Hurricane Sandy passed directly over our ship that day, as it headed first to the New Jersey shoreline and then to the coast of Long Island. As we sat comfortably aboard our ship in the bay, we could never have imagined the devastation that Sandy would ultimately cause to those only a hundred miles north of our location.

By days four and five of our adventure, we began to learn the degree of destruction to life and property that the hurricane had inflicted. Our cell phones were ringing off the hook with calls placed by family and friends who knew we were on this cruise, everyone asking how we were weathering the storm and whether we were safe.

Not only did we ride out the hurricane on this trip to nowhere yet everywhere, but we did it in the comfort of our ship, our cabin, and the facilities on board. Was it our best cruise ever? Probably not. Was it a cruise we will never forget? Undoubtedly. Would we do it again if confronted with the choice? I believe the answer is, why not?

"Opposite direction" is a term I have learned to ponder on every cruise. When making choices—not just on a cruise but also in life—will I consider alternatives to what most others are inclined to pursue? All I can say for sure is that our decision in October 2012 was one I'm glad we made. Not only did we get to tell the story about surviving a hurricane aboard a cruise ship a hundred times at the wedding, but now I have been able to share it with you as well.

Then again, if I keep telling this story, as I am prone to do, I suppose I am likely to find listeners heading in the opposite direction.

8
Captain, Director, Crew

By now, you have been well fed and have found a spot to enjoy a drink or two. You have had an opportunity to view the live entertainment and have discovered the activities in which you may choose to participate. You have explored every nook and cranny of your ship and enjoyed the peace and comfort of your cabin. Hopefully, you have also stepped ashore and visited one or more ports of call.

However you have managed your cruise, it seems likely that you are so relaxed as to have forgotten where you hid your car keys on that first day. If you are the cook in your family, you are probably delighting in how you have not touched a pot or pan since leaving home, unless of course you signed up for a cooking class aboard your ship. Cruises are magical that way.

Except here's the thing: your ability to completely relax doesn't happen by magic. Working behind the scenes is an absolutely incredible team, one carefully assembled by the cruise line to cater to your every need. Since they are so integral to the quality of your cruise, let's take a little time to meet some of these men and women, get to know them, and learn a little more about what they do and where they come from.

Let's start with an astonishing fact: for every two of us, there is one of them. That's right. For every two passengers who come aboard, there is at least one crew member there to serve us, and on some cruises, the ratio is closer to one to one. It all begins at the top with the captain and his team of officers, but make no mistake, without the crew and staff that answer to them, none of what makes this vacation so special will happen.

Over the course of your cruise, you will get to know some of the officers and crew on a first-name basis. Others you will see from a distance doing their assigned job, too busy to greet you other than with a smile or nod. It won't take you long to identify the officers, as they are always dressed in starched shirts and pants or blouses and skirts. Neither will it be difficult to identify a crew member in attire that meets the need of his or her function aboard the vessel.

It all begins on that first day when you exit the terminal to walk up the gangway for the first time. There, you will spot the crewmembers wearing T-shirts and coveralls, loading luggage and food supplies from the dock, while others perch on scaffolds to whitewash or paint the outside of the ship. Hours prior to your arrival, these crewmembers or some of their mates will have already been responsible for safely attaching the gangway to the ship and shore. They will repeat this important task at every stop along the way.

Once you have cleared security and stepped foot on the vessel, you will be greeted by men and women dressed in clothing you might expect of a cocktail waiter or waitress. They will be holding a tray bearing a refreshing welcome beverage for you to enjoy. These crewmembers are always extremely pleasant people, and it's nice to have that drink in hand as you explore your ship, so my wife and I usually accept and share a few warm words with these servers. You are likely to see one or more of them again throughout your journey as they circulate the public areas of the ship, always ready to take a drink order when the need arises.

Soon after you locate your assigned cabin, a knock on the door will give you your first chance to meet your cabin steward and his or her assistant. If by the end of your cruise, you don't know their names, where they hail from, and a little about their family, you have booked the wrong cruise. These crewmembers are certain to make your cruise as comfortable as you can imagine, so getting to know them is advisable.

After you have had a chance to unpack and freshen up, you may wish to explore the ship. You will likely meet a bar server or two assigned to a venue you may come to frequent from time to time over the course of the journey. If you are as fortunate as we have been, you may find a particular server who eventually gets to know you well enough that he or she will start making your drink before you even place your order. Israel—his name and not the country—is one fine example. We met him at the Martini Bar—the actual and not just generic name of the establishment—while exploring the ship on a Russian river cruise. We may or may not have initially selected this venue because of the promise implicit in its admittedly uninspired name, but we kept going back because of Israel.

Pro tip: If you enjoy alcoholic beverages and routine, making you the kind of person to return to a single location to drink from time to time during your cruise, getting to know your bartenders is a must. Their familiarity with you leads to better and more promptly delivered drinks. They will also appreciate your efforts to get to know them, and you will hear fascinating stories and histories that you will remember long after your cruise has ended.

Israel, for instance, was born in Nigeria before emigrating to the country of Georgia, his home situated to the south of Russia near the Black Sea. He married a Russian woman and learned a number of different languages sufficient to open the opportunity to travel abroad in the service industry. For fifteen years, Israel has tended bar on different cruise ships.

"Recently, I was promoted to the position of assistant bar manager," he told us proudly.

Israel not only knows how to make a proper dirty martini; he has proven to be a wealth of information about the ports we have visited and will be visiting, always offering plenty of insight on the must-see sights and must-take excursions. It was no accident that we sought out Israel at cocktail hour each evening, and that he always greeted us by name as he got to work placing olives and olive juice in our glasses.

Your Info-tainment Liaison

I'M GETTING AHEAD of myself a bit—dirty martinis will do that to me. We're supposed to be following the natural progression of meeting the crew on day one. So let's go back to that first day.

After the ship is fully boarded and the horn sounds advising that it is time to set sail, most of us will make our way to the open-air deck topside for the Sail Away party. Not only is this party usually quite a lot of fun; it will also serve as your first opportunity to meet your cruise director, albeit from afar, as he or she presents from the stage typically set up on or near the Lido Deck. Whatever the case, the cruise director is a person who will labor morning, noon, and night to ensure that your every expectation for a fun-filled cruise is met.

Unless the captain of your ship is more of a Captain Stubing type (for my younger readers, that's a reference to a television show called "The Love Boat," wherein the captain was uncommonly friendly and present in the experiences of his crew and passengers), your cruise director will be the most visible and perhaps the most important person on your cruise. From the morning briefing on your cabin's TV to the introduction of the evening performance in the theater, your cruise director will never be at a loss for something to do. You will see her or him poolside organizing an activity before running to a lounge to introduce you to a guest speaker. If someone needs to explain the rules, regulations, and what to expect at an upcoming port visit, you can bet the cruise director will be leading the panel.

Sometimes you will meet your captain and his or her officers during the sail-away party. Other times, this will happen at a special captain's party. Either way, you will find the cruise director standing next to the captain and his or her officers, serving as the emcee who introduces them.

Just in case that doesn't seem like enough work to you, the cruise director will also spend his or her spare time mediating problems or organizing the entertainment troupe and musical acts, all of whom she or he has helped hire on behalf of the cruise company.

A Hearty Crew

ONCE YOUR SHIP is at sea, you will undoubtedly find your way to dinner in one of the restaurants on board. Here, you will be seated and soon greeted by your waiter and assistant waiter, a duo you will come to know almost as well as your cabin steward. This is unless you opt to explore different dining venues on a regular basis.

As you are settling in to your table, a wine steward will appear and take your drink order or offer you wine from the extensive wine list placed before you. After dinner, as you wander in the direction of the theater, you may pass by the photo or art gallery, where staff members will assist you in perusing the art and/or making a purchase. Strategically positioned between the restaurants and the theater, you will find the boutiques, where more staff members will be eager to help you select from the many beautiful items on the shelves or in their jewelry cases.

If you need a little information, you might stop at guest services, where still other staff members will answer your questions, review your statement of charges, and even help you exchange currency. Somewhere in or near guest services, you will also find a station for booking excursions or even signing up for a future cruise.

You have only been aboard for several hours, and already, you have met a number of crew and staff members with very differing responsibilities. What you have not yet seen (and might never see firsthand) is the crew that works mostly behind the scenes or throughout the night while you are sound asleep dreaming about what tomorrow may hold. As an early riser, I often get to view from a distance the crew members who clean and sanitize the public areas of the ship. I wake each morning to find them vacuuming the carpets, mopping the floors, wiping down the handrails throughout, and cleaning the inside of the elevators. This cleaning effort has become more extensive in the post-COVID era. In fact, unless I'm mistaken, you don't have to rise quite so early to see the cleaning in progress anymore, as the cleaning hours begin earlier each night and extend later each morning than they used to. There seems to be quite a lot more cleaning staff on hand as well, all of them incredibly friendly and remarkably skilled at cleaning in a way that is not at all invasive to the passengers' enjoyment of the cruise.

A veritable army of crewmembers will be in the public restrooms each night and early morning, scrubbing from top to bottom, or on the outside decks swabbing the teak surfaces and cleaning the lounge chairs. On the pool deck, you will spot deckhands arranging chairs, cleaning tables, and removing safety netting from the pools and hot tubs. They will check chlorine levels, skim the pools, and do everything else necessary to keep these areas safe and clean for guests as they arrive in the hours ahead.

Whenever my early morning stroll through the ship is complete, I make my way to the buffet for a cup of coffee. This of course is where I first met Nelly, who I haven't seen in quite some time, come to think of it. Things with her new friend must be going well. In any case, my solitude as I enjoy my coffee affords the opportunity to listen to the symphony of sounds emanating from the kitchen.

Behind the various counters, crewmembers load and unload dishwashers and stand over steaming sinks. Others are busy placing items in ovens or tending to cookpots on the stovetops. Their mates fill carts with an assortment of juices, fruits, pastries, and everything else you can imagine. All around me in the dining areas, crewmembers are setting tables with silverware rolled in cloth napkins, alongside coffee cups and condiments. To me, these crewmembers are the unsung heroes who never receive a proper thank you from the guests, men and women who toil ten to twelve hours a day in the warmest places aboard the vessel, unless you find your way to the restricted areas of the ship which house the laundry and engine room. There reside other unsung heroes.

There was a time when cruise companies offered a for-fee tour of these typically restricted areas—an inside look at the "back of the house," if you will—but I have not seen that option on my present cruise, and I wonder if they will be eliminated in our post-COVID world. Hopefully not, as this tour is eye opening indeed.

Imagine what it would take to launder the towels and bedding on a ship with between 500 and 2,000 cabins, not to mention the napkins and tablecloths from the restaurants and the towels used at the different pool venues. Add to this the uniforms of the crew and the personal laundry sent out by passengers for cleaning and pressing. If ever you get a chance to see them, the laundry facilities of a cruise ship will blow your mind. The people who work in the laundry (usually with headsets over their ears allowing them to enjoy the sound of music rather than the constant and deafening roar of the machines) will never make an appearance in the public venues on the ship, and yet they will be there every day and night, at your service. It is a remarkable and often overlooked facet of cruise vacations, these incredibly hardworking people who never get to meet those whose cruises they help make so comfortable.

What do you say we visit the engine room next? On this stroll, we pass the refrigerators and freezers that protect perishable foods from spoilage during the cruise. You might also notice the storage shelves that hold the cans and dry goods necessary to round out your meals.

If on the first day of your cruise, you came aboard early in the day, you might have noticed members of the kitchen crew loading the ship portside. They have their work cut out for them. To give you an idea of how large an area of the ship they will have packed with food, consider that a seven-day cruise carrying 1,950 passengers and 990 crew members (which would have been a vanishingly small number pre-COVID but has become closer to the norm these days) will be packed with 24,236 pounds of beef, 5,040 pounds of lamb, 7,216 pounds of pork, 4,600 pounds of veal, 1,680 pounds of sausage, 10,211 pounds of chicken, and 3,156 pounds of turkey. If you prefer fish to meat or just want to change it up from time to time, the ship will have 13,851 pounds of fish, 2,100 pounds of lobster, and a mere 350 pounds of crab to keep you satisfied. Why so little crab compared to lobster? Search me.

Okay, so you're a vegetarian. You won't go hungry either, as the assortment of greens and veggies of other colors will never leave you wanting. The ship is bearing 25,736 pounds of fresh vegetables, 20,003 pounds of fresh fruit, and 15,150 pounds of potatoes, presumably to serve as ballast for the ship as well as ballast for our bodies.

Do you have a sweet tooth? Not to worry. Rolling aboard came 600 gallons of ice cream, 1,926 quarts of cream, 5,750 pounds of sugar, and 1,936 pounds of cookies. I am not quite sure why cookies were brought aboard, as the pastry chef and his talented crew spend hours each day and night baking homemade cakes, pies, tortes, and puddings, not to forget donuts, pastries, croissants, and muffins, which will be served straight from the oven at 6:00 a.m. when the buffet opens for breakfast.

Speaking of breakfast, those heroic crewmembers also loaded onto the vessel 9,235 dozen eggs, 1,750 pounds of jelly, 2,458 pounds of coffee, and 3,260 gallons of milk. They have also stored sufficient amounts of flour to make pancakes, blintzes, and crepes to complement your made-to-order omelet. Somehow, butter was never mentioned in my research, which leaves me to wonder if the American Medical Association asked that the amount of butter remain undisclosed. Suffice to say, you will never run out of butter on your cruise.

Let's not forget the drinks either. Coming aboard was an ample amount of alcoholic beverages, including 3,400 bottles of wine, 200 bottles of champagne, 200 bottles of gin, 290 bottles of vodka, 350 bottles of whiskey, 150 bottles of rum, 45 bottles of sherry, 600 bottles of assorted liquors, and for our old friend Archie, 10,100 bottles of beer.

If you ever have the opportunity to meet one of the crewmembers who helped port all of these goods onto the ship, be sure to thank him or her—maybe even with one of those 10,100 beers, if the ship's rules allow—as none of this would have been possible without those efforts.[2]

It seems to be taking a long time to get to the engine room, doesn't it? This is because we have yet to pass by

---

2 en.wikipedia.org/wiki/Provisioning_(cruise_ship)

the main kitchens and prep areas of the ship, where the hundreds of thousands of pounds of food from these freezers, refrigerators, and shelves are made ready to be transported up the dumbwaiters to the serving stations. Here, you will see kitchen staff washing and separating lettuce; peeling shrimp; and trimming sides of beef. We're walking at such a rapid clip now that I can't even begin to count the crewmembers working at these various stations.

Finally, we've arrived at the engine room, and it's immediately clear to see why not all uniforms stay clean and white as the day progresses. Hard at work are the men and women who keep this vessel in operating condition. Of course, we live in a technologically advanced world, where computers do much of our work, but it still takes a human hand to apply the grease, change the oil, and seal the pipes. The engine rooms of today look nothing like the engine rooms I observed in my early days of cruising, but they remain a fascinating place to visit if you ever get the chance.

You Might Be Compelled to Salute

NOW THAT YOU have met many of the members of your crew, let's get acquainted with the officers who supervise them, beginning with your captain. If you—like I used to—are envisioning an old man of the sea with long white hair, a beard to match, and a corncob pipe in his teeth, I'm sorry to disappoint. He or she probably won't even have an eyepatch or a parrot perched on the shoulder either.

The captains of today are typically much younger than the stereotype. Some are men and some are women, and they are always healthy, sharp, and in tip-top shape. On the subject of genders, you might be startled to learn that it wasn't until the year 2007 that the title of cruise ship captain could go to a woman. This was when Karin Stahre-Janson from Sweden made history by becoming the first woman to captain a mega-cruise ship. She began her career with a bachelor's degree in Nautical Sciences before serving first as a junior seaman on a petroleum tanker and working her way up the ranks. Then, in 2007, she took command of Royal Caribbean's *Monarch of the Seas*, a 74,000-ton vessel capable of carrying 2,700-plus passengers and a crew of well over a thousand.

In the earliest days of cruising, captains hailed from seafaring nations like Norway, Denmark, Sweden, the United Kingdom, Italy, and Greece. But since the turn of the twenty-first century, captains from the United States, Russia, South America, Australia, and many other parts of the world joined this exclusive club. In 2015, Kate McCue became the first female captain from the United States when she was awarded command of the *Celebrity*

Summit from Celebrity Cruise Lines. Today, she captains the *Celebrity Edge*, a 130,000-ton vessel with a passenger capacity of 2,900 and a crew of over 1,200. This ship also prides itself on being the first ever cruise ship to employ an entirely female group of bridge officers.

The racial barriers for women were broken in 2016, when Belinda Bennett was named captain of the *MSY Windstar*, a four-masted sailing ship that sails the Caribbean Sea during the winter months and travels to exotic ports of call around the world for the remainder of the year. Born on the island of St. Helena off the coast of Africa, Captain Bennett rose through the ranks to get to where she is today. This is also true of the fifteen other women who captain cruise ships from an inventory of over three hundred sailing the seas. There are likely to be more women captains by the time you pick up this book, and you can bet that they will all be worth a Google search, as their careers are always fascinating.

The role of a cruise-ship captain has changed somewhat in the modern era of technological advancement, but we must never underestimate the value of having a top-shelf captain guide us on our journey out to sea. Just consider what decisions the three-hundred-plus captains on the seas had to have made when the COVID pandemic first reared its ugly head. The same can be said of the excellent captain who guided us into Chesapeake Bay during Hurricane Sandy.

When a ship must advise its passengers it will not be docking at a port because of civil unrest (which happens from time to time), it is the captain who has made that difficult yet wise decision. If a person suffers a serious life-threatening event while the ship is at sea, it is the captain who will lead him or her to a safe place for treatment.

We may see our captain out and about socializing with passengers during our cruise far more frequently than in the past, but you can rest assured that he is on the bridge when the ship is approaching or leaving port.

Captains of today's vessels are ably assisted by a cadre of officers who are trained in every aspect of operating the vessel, from engineering to hotel management and everything between. Take, for instance, the hotel manager I was able to meet and converse with at a Captain's Party a few cruises ago.

The Hotel Manager

ON A CRUISE where we were enjoying a suite, my wife and I were invited, along with a small number of other guests, to enjoy cocktails in the captain's quarters, where we would get a chance to meet some of the officers and learn more about them and the duties they perform during a cruise. Naturally, we leapt at the opportunity.

Not long after we arrived for the well-appointed affair,

I noticed a woman in a white uniform with enough stripes on her shoulders to indicate she had an important job. I approached and introduced myself.

With a pleasant smile, she introduced herself as Mary Hopkins, the ship's hotel manager. She hailed from Madison, Wisconsin, and had earned her undergraduate and master's degrees in hotel management at Cornell University in Ithaca, New York. She had been serving in her present role for the past five years. She had not come into this role by chance, however. Rather, it was her experience managing at various resorts and hotels throughout the world that earned her the opportunity.

"You're certainly decorated as a high-ranking officer," I said, gesturing to her shoulder stripes. "I'd be interested to hear more about your duties."

"Where should I begin?" She took a deep breath. "Each morning, I begin my rounds at 6:00 a.m. Rounds start with observing the public areas of the ship to ensure they're clean and ready to receive guests. From the buffet, I work my way through the dining rooms and lounges before heading to my office to sort through some paperwork."

At first, I found myself slightly disappointed with this answer, but it seemed that the description of her day had only just begun.

"At about 8:00 a.m.," she continued, "I head to the decks where the cabins are located to make sure the cabin stewards are doing their jobs. I may even pop into a room or two for inspection before returning to my office, where I will have a light breakfast."

"So it seems like there's quite a bit of office time."

"My job does involve a lot of paperwork, yes. My department orders all the towels, bed linens, soaps, and sundry items you require in your cabin, including the toilet paper. We purchase all the tablecloths, napkins, silverware, and glasses used aboard the ship. Our department is also responsible for replenishing the cleaning supplies our staff uses. Oh! I almost forgot. We also purchase the uniforms for our crew."

Okay, I thought. *So I'm dealing with a purchasing agent. There must be more to this job.*

Mary confirmed my suspicion. "Our department hires, trains, disciplines, and from time to time, must discharge some of the more than eighty percent of the people who work on this ship. Under my supervision are the head of the housekeeping department and the food-and-beverage manager, along with their hundreds of employees."

Now we were getting somewhere. "Discipline and discharge?" I asked, intrigued.

She smiled. "For obvious reasons, I'm prohibited from speaking about specific cases. But I can tell you that among the nine hundred or so people we employ, problems sometimes arise. We're tasked with resolving them. Our staff comes from no fewer than twenty different countries, so the cultural differences and language barriers can sometimes raise issues between individual staff members."

"It's got to be challenging communicating with everyone if they don't all speak the same language."

"I'm fortunate to be fluent in English and Spanish, but my understanding of Russian and Mandarin is minimal at best. Thankfully, most of our Filipino and Indonesian staff speak English. Many other countries have adopted English as their second language, so we're usually able to navigate our communication with little support."

"I have to say, I'm still wondering about those disciplinary issues…"

She shrugged. "Some are straightforward, like tardiness or the appearance of a crew member's uniform. Others involve crewmember interactions, whether with each other or with guests. If one crewmember oversteps the bounds of appropriate behavior with another crewmember, we'll deal with that behind closed doors. It's when a crewmember and a guest have an issue that presents the greatest challenge."

I couldn't help myself. "Such as?"

"Let's just say the old saying, 'The customer is always right,' may not always be the case. On occasion, we may reassign a cabin steward or change the table at which a waiter works. These are the easy cases. From time to time, alcohol will cause a guest to say something inappropriate to a crewmember. This is when I look for help from my captain. Social interaction between crew and guests is strictly prohibited, and yet this has been known to occur. Unless the crewmember avoids this, he or she will be on their way home at the next port we enter."

"That's fascinating," I said, the gears already turning on how this information would fit nicely into the book.

"Please don't think me rude," Mary said pleasantly, "but I see the captain waving for me to join him."

"By all means!" I stepped aside to let her through. "Please don't let me keep you."

"I've enjoyed meeting you," she said. "I hope you continue to have a wonderful cruise."

The hasty nature of her exit from the conversation served as further evidence that the position of hotel manager was worthy of every stripe on her uniform.

Not far from where we had been standing, I noticed a burly gentleman with an equal number of shoulder stripes. He happened to be holding court with several other guests, but I did manage to eavesdrop enough to overhear that he was the chief engineer, responsible for things like clean drinking water, plumbing, electrical power, and engine thrust. As a man who sits at a desk most of the day and depends on his wife to fix everything mechanical and electrical at home, I knew I was way out of my league in understanding much of what he seemed to be relating to the guests surrounding him. Later in the voyage, I would spot him in grease-stained coveralls, leading an entourage of crewmembers with wrenches, flashlights, and an assortment of other tools as they hustled to their next task. It was only then that I came to appreciate the awesome responsibility of the chief engineer of an 800-foot ship in the 140,000-ton class of cruise vessels.

As the gathering drew toward its conclusion, the captain thanked us for attending, then invited us all to take in a lecture in the theater the following morning hosted by his staff captain. I promised myself I would be in attendance.

The Staff Captain

FLASH FORWARD TO the next morning, when, at 10:00 a.m. sharp, every seat available in the theater was filled with guests. At the microphone sitting center stage was a woman in a starched white uniform with even more shoulder stripes than the hotel manager and chief engineer. She introduced herself as Elizabeth Thielman, the staff captain of our ship. In the ensuing hour, I learned that the staff captain is second in command of the vessel and serves as the eyes and ears of the captain.

If you follow American politics, you'll know that in order to meet with the president you must first get permission from the chief of staff. The same can be said of the working relationship between the captain and his or her staff captain. Every officer on board the ship answers to the captain through the staff captain. More important, however, is that the staff captain must be able to assume the duties of the captain at any given moment, or in the event that an emergency prevents the captain from performing his or her duties. In addition, it is the staff captain who oversees all activities on the bridge during docking and other maneuvers, such as anchoring, departures from a port, and command of the navigation of the vessel while in open seas.

Working directly under the supervision of the staff captain are the first, second, and third officers, whose titles are a bit misleading. These three officers man the bridge twenty-four hours a day in shifts, and one of the three is always on duty whether in port or at sea.

The staff captain supervises the actions of the chief engineer and bears ultimate responsibility for the fresh-water supply of the ship and its safe consumption. The training of all officers, crew, and staff in emergency procedures falls within his or her remit, and this officer will supervise safety drills aboard on a daily basis. Further, it is the staff captain's job to ensure that all safety equipment, including life preservers and lifeboats, are in excellent working condition in the event the need arises for their use.

If there is an accident on board involving either a passenger or a crewmember, it is the staff captain who investigates the incident, writes a report, and hopefully resolves the matter to the satisfaction of everyone involved. Standing orders on a ship are to be followed strictly, and the staff captain will make certain this occurs. In her spare time, Staff Captain Thielman would schedule visits to the bridge for passengers lucky enough to be invited to view the ship's nerve center firsthand. This particular lecture, however, would be one of only two times she would make an official appearance before guests. The other would be during a special dinner she would host in the dining room later in the week. Other than this, she wouldn't have much opportunity to lounge around the ship, as time isn't something a person in this role can spare. Their daily responsibilities never seem to end.

In my admittedly nonlinear way, I have now introduced you to the top four officers of this ship: the captain, the staff captain, the hotel manager, and the chief engineer. Although not given a uniform with stripes on the shoulders, your cruise director certainly ranks right up there with these officers, even though he or she answers to the hotel manager in the chain of command.

And let's not pass over the many other fine officers who serve our many and diverse needs during the voyage. I am referring first to the doctors and nurses, who also wear uniforms. Also of note is the purser of the ship, who, as his or her title suggests, supervises the ship's purse as well as the ship's manifest, including passports and documentation that allow the ship to enter each and every port of call. Not unlike in the military, everyone has a specific duty to perform and is accountable up and down the chain of command.

Before we move forward in our exploration of the people we meet and get to know during a typical cruise vacation, I'd like to wrap up this chapter with a few asides about your crew and officers that may help you to appreciate them even more. These tidbits make up my list of top fun encounters I have been privileged to experience over the course of my many cruises.

> Yes, I was asked by a passenger if she could marry her cabin steward and have him debark with her in Miami.

> I never grew tired of the look on the face of our many waiters over the years after my dear friend Doug had ordered everything on the menu.

> Once, our captain gave a speech about not having time to meet and greet every passenger on the ship. He said this in front of the parents of a young woman who had been gifted this cruise as a college graduation present. Later, as those parents prepared to leave the ship after their final day of the cruise, they were stunned to learn that the captain himself had

invited their daughter to stay as his personal guest for another week of cruising.

Last but not least was the cruise director's imitation of Elaine Bettis's dancing, as depicted in an episode of "Seinfeld." I can only hope it was an imitation and not the real thing.

One last thought before we leave our introduction to your officers and crew: a word of heartfelt thanks and appreciation goes out to all of you for the way you navigated your lives through this pandemic. As first responders, you sacrificed yourselves for the safety of your passengers. Next, you endured months of isolation away from home and family while trapped aboard your ships sailing to nowhere. Now, we get to reunite as we together venture out to do what we all love to do.

9
This Isn't a Private Yacht

So you have the food and drink; your cabin and the public venues; the entertainment and activities on board; and the visits to ports of call. If you're anything like my wife and me, these many elements will seem so personally tailored to you and your traveling companion/family that you might sometimes start to think you're on a private yacht with an itinerary designed specifically with you (and only you) in mind. We know how you feel. We've certainly been there. It's a remarkable thing, especially considering that most cruises have hundreds if not thousands of other passengers aboard.

Trust me, the other people are there. In fact, getting to know them, at least from a distance, is one of the best parts about cruising. People-watching is most everyone's favorite sport, and I can tell you without hesitation that there is no better place in the world to people-watch than on a cruise. You've already met Nelly and Doug, Easygoing Eddie and Energetic Eve, and Archie and his poor wife, so we'll skim past them on our own little people-watching excursion and instead delve into a few other personalities you can expect to encounter, no matter where in the world you decide to cruise.

The game begins in the terminal as you stand in line waiting to check in and receive your room keys and important instructions. You might spot the guy in the print shirt, the one eating a submarine sandwich, or the woman berating her husband and/or children for not having their passports in hand.

Panning back, you might also notice the general demographic makeup of your fellow travelers. On some cruises, they might look younger than you. On others, the crowd might seem a tad further on in years than you happen to be at the time. It's the strangest thing; I've noticed that this latter possibility becomes decreasingly likely for me every time we cruise.

You might also consider the general quality of everyone's manner of dress, or how they conduct themselves while waiting in line. Are they patient, or do they seem to be in a hurry? What are their projectable levels of stress?

On the subject of stress, I've noticed over the years that you can tell a lot about a person based on how they comport themselves when faced with stress. Checking in to any cruise vacation tends to be the most stressful time for most people—particularly newcomers to the cruise getaway—and in the face of this, people tend to show a different side of themselves.

Since it's always so much fun to watch, let's start there.

When Boarding a Cruise Ties You in Knots

FIRST MEET Bill and Barbara, friends of mine for many years. Later, we'll meet Nosy Nelly's cousins, Nervous Nelly and her husband Ned. Both of them are fictitious characters, but their story is likely one with which you'll be able to identify.

For Barbara's fortieth birthday, Bill decided to surprise her with a seven-day cruise to Bermuda and back. My old friend pulled out all the stops, even renting a limousine to bear them from their home to the airport. When he alighted from the limo in his driveway, he found Barbara dressed in a pair of shorts and a top she typically reserved for doing a bit of gardening in the yard.

"What's going on?" She had a puzzled look on her face.

Beaming, Bill leveled his wife with the surprise. "Stop what you're doing and go into the house," he said excitedly. "Wash up and throw an overnight bag together. We're heading out on an adventure."

"Where are we going?" Barbara's tone, it seems, was already less enthusiastic than Bill had anticipated. "And what should I bring?"

"Just bring a nightgown and put on a nice blouse and slacks. That's all you'll need."

Barbara and Bill had been married for close to twenty years, so she was used to him pulling rabbits out of hats. But this was a whole new level of rabbit. Still, she complied. They climbed into the limo, which drove them to the airport, where they boarded a plane for New York City. As you can imagine, Barbara was totally confused by this point.

"What are we doing when we get to New York? I have nothing to wear."

"Don't worry, honey! Tomorrow morning, you can shop up and down Fifth Avenue and buy whatever you'll need for a week in the sun. You might want to get something for when we go out to dinner. And don't forget to buy a bathing suit."

Upon their arrival in New York, the taxi headed for Manhattan, eventually pulling up in front of the Four Seasons Hotel. If nothing else, the adventure had started off in style. It was then that Barbara asked why she would need a bathing suit to tour Manhattan.

"We're only staying in New York overnight and part of tomorrow. Then we're moving on to our next destination. Trust me! You won't be disappointed."

Bill is a very brave man.

Or perhaps he could just count himself fortunate to have married a lovely woman willing to put so much trust in her husband's judgment. Still, though, this one might have been pushing the envelope a bit further than usual.

After a full three hours at Saks, Bergdorf Goodman, and Bloomingdales, Barbara looked like Julia Roberts on Rodeo Drive in "Pretty Woman." They hailed a cab, filled the trunk with her purchases, and headed for the West Side Cruise Terminal, where the nature of the adventure came into focus for her.

"We're boarding this beautiful ship and heading to Bermuda for your birthday," Bill announced with a smile of extreme satisfaction.

You have to hand it to my friend. He had arranged the entire trip without Barbara having even an inkling that something was being planned to celebrate her fortieth. Bill had arranged for a neighbor to move into their house and watch their teenage girls, and even the girls had been kept in the dark about his plans.

When they boarded the ship, they were ushered to a lovely suite where a chilled bottle of champagne greeted them, along with an arrangement of red roses and a few balloons imprinted with the words, "Happy 40th."

Now, that's certainly a low-stress way to travel from home to the cabin of your ship. I wonder...what does the other end of the spectrum look like?

Nervous Nelly and Nervous Ned better describe what most of us experience before embarking on a cruise vacation. We plan, and then we plan some more. And even then, all the planning does little to assuage the tension involved in getting from home, to the airport, to the port, through check-in, and to the first sweet, relaxing lounger and/or beverage aboard the ship.

"Honey! Did you notify the post office and newspaper delivery people to hold our mail and paper?"

"Uh huh."

"Are you sure we've left sufficient instructions for the babysitter?"

"Uh huh."

"Does everyone know how to reach us in an emergency?"

"Uh huh."

These are just a few of the exchanges you may find yourself having as the days or even hours before your departure dwindle away. Next comes the luggage from the basement and the process of selecting appropriate clothing for the trip.

"Do I need to pack a dress or evening gown?"

"Yes. Will I need a sport coat?"

"Well, if I need a dress, you need a sport coat. And be sure to pack more than one bathing suit."

"Why? Are you packing more than one?"

"Of course I'm packing more than one. It's a week in the sun, and people will be watching what we wear."

"What do you think the temperature will be?"

"Hot. How about our passports and boarding passes?

Do you know where those are?"

"Of course I do."

"Should I bring my computer, or will my iPad be sufficient?"

"Are you planning on working?"

"Maybe."

"This is vacation. Leave the computer at home."

"Should I bring a lot of cash? And which credit cards will be accepted?"

Well. You get the idea.

Once you board your ship and sit poolside with a refreshing drink surrounded by others of like mind, I guarantee you will not be able to pick out who are Bill and Barbara and who are Nelly and Ned. The pre-cruise stress will be long gone, and both couples—along with the rest of us—will now be able to enjoy what lies ahead.

The same may not prove true for the family of ten you will meet tonight in the dining room as they are ushered to the table next to you.

You're Traveling with How Many Children?

NOT EVERYONE ON your cruise will be as gregarious and perhaps annoying as Nosy Nelly and your author. Many guests will keep to themselves or the family and friends accompanying them, but these passengers are equally worthy of mention as they, too, will play an important role in how well you enjoy your cruise vacation. After all, depending on the size of the vessel or where in the world it is sailing, you will no doubt see many of these people on an almost daily basis.

Take, for instance, the three-generations-strong family seated at the table next to me at dinner one evening in the dining room. Though we didn't speak to them directly, it seemed that Grandma and Grandpa had gone to great lengths and expense to bring the family together for a week at sea, as it gave them an opportunity to enjoy quality time with the people they loved most. The table was set for ten, and a quick look in that direction led me to believe that those seats not belonging to Grandma and Grandpa were occupied by two of their children, each with a spouse. The four younger faces at the table could only belong to the grandkids.

This was where the fun began for a people-watcher like me. Without staring at them, I attempted to determine which of the adults were the children of Grandma and Grandpa, which were the spouses, and which kids belonged to whom. Facial similarities are usually a starting point in this game, but it doesn't take long to insert mannerisms and verbal interaction into the equation. Within a few seconds, I identified the mother of at least two of the children, as she issued directives to a cute little girl and her mischievous little brother, who had just hidden his sister's silverware under his napkin.

The look on Grandpa's face, along with the stern words he uttered to the mother to "Let the kids be kids," solved the question of which of the two in this couple was his daughter.

But which of the men was her husband? The one so engaged in his salad and soup that he didn't even look up? Or was it the second gentleman, who was engaged in heated conversation with the other woman seated next to him? My first impression was that the husband was too busy eating to be bothered by the interaction, and that the other man had to have been talking to his wife. I was proven wrong when the second woman told the man seated next to her that his children weren't behaving properly and that he should be of a little more help to his wife.

Within three or four minutes at most, I was able to solve the puzzle, even though hardly a word had been spoken. It was at this moment that my wife reminded me to stop eavesdropping and get back to eating my meal.

"You're right," I said. "Sorry."

Now that I had actually turned my focus to the food, I found that it was incredible. Onion soup, creamy mashed potatoes, a filet, and some of those for-some-reason-less-popular crab legs. A comfort meal if ever there was one. Sign me up for that any day.

Throughout the cruise, I observed this family of ten, sometimes all together and other times in smaller segments. I'd spot them enjoying themselves at the swimming pool; exiting the ship to visit a port; or just in passing on one of the decks. In spite of first impressions, this family proved itself as unobtrusive as any couple who quietly goes about their cruise.

The same may not be said of the family we met on a Christmas cruise we booked a few short years ago, traveling from Ft. Lauderdale to the eastern Caribbean and back. This cruise taught us that this is a time of year when families are more likely to cruise together than at any other. It makes perfect sense, considering the children are on school break and the parents are more easily able to take time off from work. Cruising as a couple, my wife and I were able to sit back and observe how these families enjoyed or did not enjoy being together for ten days in a somewhat confined space.

We saw how grandparents doted over their grandchildren, while Mom and Dad often found places to hide from the kids. We surmised that in many cases, Grandma and Grandpa were footing the entire cost of the cruise. Some of the younger children did what younger children tend to do: they ran around the ship, chasing each other, with little or no supervision. The preteen children seemed to enjoy the cruise in much the way we were enjoying it, by taking in the sights and the beauty of the ship, which was decorated with trees, wreaths, and garlands.

If there was a time of day when we wished to distance ourselves from the many families on board, it was during cocktail hour, when we like to sit at a bar, have a drink, and listen to the pianist play a few songs. Unfortunately, on this cruise, it became a time when a teenager or two would attempt to convince the bartender that they were twenty-one and not seventeen, eighteen, or nineteen. Some of the time, this occurred while the parents and grandparents enjoyed their cocktails in a different lounge or at a different bar. Occasionally, this took place under the watchful—or not so watchful—eye of their parents, some of whom even tried to order their teenagers' drinks for them.

I try not to judge how others act, and our concern was more for the bartender, who has a job to protect, both for himself and for the guests aboard the ship. We learned soon enough that on this cruise, it would be better to enjoy cocktail hour on the balcony of our stateroom for the duration of the voyage.

In fairness to the majority of families traveling alongside us, most of the time the family members were having a pleasant family vacation, and the age differential between them and us went unnoticed. I happen to be a grandparent to seven grandchildren whose company I enjoy for a few hours at a time or even an occasional overnight or two. In fact, I enjoy my time with them immensely. Still, I don't believe I have the intestinal fortitude to spend ten days and nights with them on a cruise—or for that matter, any other type of vacation.

Our lesson learned after that cruise was that it is probably more peaceful for a couple our age to spend the holiday season somewhere other than on a cruise ship. I add this to a lesson learned much earlier in life, when we figured out the hard way that some cruises are better reserved for the younger set. I refer to what you might call a "Party Cruise."

Are You Ready for a Party?

THE THEME SONG of Monday Night Football loudly wonders, "Are you ready for some football?" A commercial for a three-day-and-night cruise from Miami to the Bahamas and back would ask, "Are you ready for a party?"

Since the onset of COVID-19, you have surely seen pictures and videos of thousands of people partying at a beach bar despite social distancing warnings from the CDC. All you have to do to form a picture of what a three-day cruise to nowhere looks like is to move that beach-bar imagery to a cruise ship leaving Miami on a Friday afternoon. Age differentials will not matter on such a cruise. The only thing that will matter is whether your body can tolerate the toll that three days and nights of partying will take on you.

When I was a lot younger than I am today, I could stand toe to toe with passengers enjoying their three-day weekend on the high seas. I even learned a few first names of the people I spilled my beer on, assuming they were actually telling me their real names. The only mistake I made was in not allowing that memory to remain a memory.

A few years ago, a friend and I attempted to relive our youth by again joining guests boarding a similar cruise. It took time to load the ship—not with luggage, as luggage would have been as unnecessary as bringing along a book to read. What took so long to load was the outrageous amount of alcohol necessary to keep everyone's thirst sated for three days. If I had to guess, I would imagine that my friend and I were among the few who actually slept in the stateroom we had been assigned.

As I emerged from the cabin to have breakfast each morning, I was careful not to step on or bump into a body sleeping it off along my path to the buffet. By noon, the party would be back in full swing, the music blasting out of speakers throughout the ship.

Being a people-watcher, I made sure to be among the first to disembark on Monday morning, so that I might linger in the terminal and catch a glimpse of the varied degrees of hangover departing the ship. I wasn't disappointed. I've never seen so many different shades of green.

Open Seas, Open Eyes

IF YOU EVER have the opportunity to cross the Atlantic on a fourteen-day repositioning cruise, you will find that people-watching takes a bit more concentration on this kind of voyage, as one must attempt to envision what one's fellow passengers have done in life to bring them aboard the ship. One thing that all will have in common is their willingness to stay aboard a cruise vessel for fourteen days, with only a couple of stops along the way.

People who love sailing across an ocean tend to be quite different from those willing to endure a three-day party cruise. They will undoubtedly be a tad older, but in today's world, with people retiring at such young ages, you will see and perhaps even meet guests in their forties and fifties. As you stroll by the swimming pool, you will notice a fair number of guests reading a book, gazing at a magazine, or listening to music on their headphones.

Most passengers who sail on these voyages do so for very personal reasons. Some come aboard to take care of a frail spouse or parent. Some travel alone or with a companion to cleanse their minds of problems they have left behind. Others are looking to what the future may hold for them. My wife and I cross the ocean because we love the feel of sea air, an opportunity to catch up on some reading, watch a few movies, and to exercise in the fitness center—all of which we seldom find time to do at home. It will not surprise you to learn that a fourteen-day cruise affords me an opportunity to write without finding excuses not to do so as well.

Some people who cruise the seas enjoy socializing and

meeting new people. Others travel with family members or close friends and prefer to spend quality time together. Some, like my wife and me, enjoy quiet time alone. As different as we all are, we have one very important thing in common: we have all come aboard because we chose to. No one has forced us to do this. To steal a line from the movie "Patton," we do it because we love it.

My Own Rose Dawson

ROSE DAWSON CAME aboard the Titanic in Southampton, England, as a spoiled young lady who had been betrothed by her struggling and lonely mother to marry a wealthy tycoon. Rose left the Titanic, sadly not in New York, only a few days after setting sail, a grown-up and self-sufficient woman because of her fortuitous meeting with a young Jack Dawson, who had won his chance to sail across the Atlantic Ocean in a card game moments before the ship was set to leave port.

We all know what happened to the Titanic, but we can only surmise what happened to Rose, who took the name Dawson during the seventy years between being rescued—both from the ship and her arranged marriage—until we met her again in the movie which recounts that ill-fated voyage.

My Rose Dawson is a woman I had the pleasure to meet while cruising to Bermuda a few years ago. It was lunchtime on the ship, and the buffet restaurant was beginning to fill up with hungry passengers, some coming from the pool area and others from a lecture in the theater. At this time of day, seats tend to be at a premium. One would be wise to locate a vacant table immediately upon arrival. While my wife was perusing the food offerings, I noticed a lady sitting by herself at a table that would typically accommodate four diners. I do not know for certain what possessed me to ask her if my wife and I might join her. She welcomed us to her table with a beautiful smile.

Ever since childhood, I have been drawn to people who have achieved senior status. I learned early in life that young children and elder men and women are never to blame for the shortcomings of our world. Rather, it is all of us in between that cause the problems we must daily confront. The welcoming smile of my Rose Dawson should have been enough to let me know that this was going to be a lunch to remember.

"Grab a seat, young man, before it is too late, and I will put my jacket on the chair next to me so your wife will have a seat as well. People gobble these seats up in a big hurry at lunchtime."

"Thank you for the invitation," I said. "I'm certain my wife will find us before too long."

"Well I hope your wife's not the jealous type," she said with a smirk.

I laughed. "I'm pretty sure she'll be pleased with my table selection."

Soon, I would learn that my own Rose Dawson's true name was Florence Reid, though she will forever remain Rose in my mind.

"So, Ms. Reid," I said as I took my seat, "where is home for you?"

"For the past three months, right here on this ship. And I'll be here another couple of months if I'm lucky not to cause enough trouble to be booted off. If you know what I mean..."

"I cannot imagine what you could possibly do to have that happen," I was saying as my wife approached the table with her usual smile and a plate of food from the buffet. "Honey!" I said. "This is Ms. Reid, and she has been kind enough to welcome us to her table. I think I'll get a sandwich and some soup while you two get acquainted."

When I returned, my wife and Ms. Reid were in animated conversation, my wife having spent so much time talking and laughing that she hadn't even touched her food.

"I hate to interrupt you," I said, "but what are you telling my wife to make her laugh? She doesn't always like the tablemates I select."

Ms. Reid shrugged. "Your wife thinks I'm funny, I guess."

"Not just funny, Ms. Reid," my wife interjected. "You're both charming and hysterical."

"I'm glad you think so. My kids and grandchildren and even the older great-grandchildren think I'm a bit crazy to spend so much time at sea." She leaned forward and gave me a conspiratorial eye. "If it's all right with you, I was telling your bride how I came to love cruising and the life aboard a cruise ship. And by the way, I am ninety-one years young, in case you were wondering. I thought I'd tell you that before you asked."

It was becoming apparent to me that today's lunch was going to take a lot longer than most of our lunches, and I was in no hurry to move along to other afternoon activities. Ms. Reid was not only going to entertain us, but she already had earned a place in this book and in my heart.

"Well that's nice to know," I said. "And so you're aware, we're in no hurry. So please regale us with the story."

"You may not be in a hurry, but I have a lot to do between now and dinner. There's a movie I want to watch at two; then I get my hair done at four; I'll get dressed up for dinner tonight because they're serving steak and lobster in the dining room; and if I time it right, I'll be able to enjoy a martini before dinner."

I drew a breath to ask if she ever took time to relax on these cruises. Instead, I decided not to interrupt.

"Where was I?" she said. "In case I didn't tell you, I'm ninety-one, and sometimes I forget where I left off."

"You were telling us how much you love to cruise," I offered.

"Oh dear! It's a bit of a tale, but I'll do my best to remember some of the details. My first husband died suddenly of a heart attack in his forties. He worked for Ford Motor Company in Detroit on the assembly line. He and I had three children, but he never had the chance to know any of our seven grandchildren and twelve great-grandchildren."

In unison, my wife and I expressed our condolences.

"Save the tears for later, as that was only the beginning of my story. After Jack died—" I knew his name would be Jack—"I moved to Florida to escape the cold winters. I met a gentleman a few years later, one who had owned and sold a lumber company. He was about my age, and it sure didn't hurt that he had a few bucks in the bank. Kyle liked the finer things in life, and lucky for me, he liked me as well. We were married, and our honeymoon was my introduction to cruising. Kyle loved to cruise, and it didn't take me very long to learn to love it as well."

"Ms. Reid," I said, "I'm sorry to interrupt, but could I get you something to drink? Maybe an iced tea or a lemonade?"

"No thanks, but if you can flag down the wine steward, I might enjoy a glass of chardonnay."

We were all so engaged that I opted for a bottle with three glasses. The wine steward didn't know my wife or me, but as soon as he approached the table, he greeted our new friend with a "Good afternoon, Ms. Reid."

"Good afternoon, Rodger," she said. "You know what to bring me, yes?"

Rodger certainly appeared to know what to bring her, as off he went.

"Anyway," Ms. Reid said, returning to her story as if she had never been interrupted, "we kept cruising at least two or three times a year until Kyle passed away two years ago. He had a terrible cancer but cruised right up until the last month of his life. It was then that I decided to cruise most of the year. He left me quite well off, in case you want to charge the wine to my account."

"Where have you cruised?" my wife asked.

"We cruised most of the world, but now I try to take cruises that periodically stop in Ft. Lauderdale in case I need to attend to things at home. I still have a condo there, and from time to time, I like to check in with the kids to let them know I'm still kicking."

I wanted to ask if she got off the ship at the various ports along the route, along with a million other questions about how one manages a whole life on a cruise ship, but I was afraid I might wear her out and ruin the rest of her well-planned day. She must have read my mind, because she informed me that she would be skipping the movie and was now free until 4:00 p.m. She had no intention of skipping the hair appointment, however, and she made that very clear.

"Call me Florence, by the way," she said, "because 'Ms. Reid' makes me feel old."

"Are you getting off in Bermuda?" I asked.

"No! I'm skipping the movie today because I've seen it several times, but I've seen Bermuda twice as many times as that. Besides, the drinks in Bermuda, like everything else, are outrageously priced."

"Do you ever get off the ship?"

"Every once in a while, I get the urge to stretch my legs, and usually a good Samaritan steps forward and lets me tag along. I'm reluctant to venture out alone, but if I had a strong guy like you to walk next to and hold his arm, I probably would get off, even in Bermuda tomorrow despite the cost of the drinks."

I felt certain that my wife was happy to learn that I had a new woman in my life, and she looked forward to tomorrow as much as I did.

"Florence, have you ever seen the movie 'Titanic'?"

"You know, I wasn't born yesterday. I think I told you I'm ninety-one years old. Of course I have seen 'Titanic'—and at least a few times. They don't show it on cruise ships, though, if you know what I mean."

"I ask because you remind me of Rose Dawson."

"Then call me Rose, for goodness sake, and pour me a little more chardonnay while you're at it."

How could you not fall in love with Florence Reid?

One of the truly wonderful things about taking a cruise

vacation is the number of men and women well up in years you will meet on your voyage. It is no secret that the cruise industry thrives on the volume of seniors who sail on their ships. A piece of advice: get to know one or two of them while you're on your journey. You might just find yourself engaged in a conversation you will remember for the rest of your life.

Watch Your Gaze

FROM TIME TO time on any given cruise, you will see a rather mature-looking man walking hand in hand with a woman at least half his age. If truth be told, you may see this more frequently than you might expect. Is it Dad vacationing with his daughter? I try to give everyone the benefit of the doubt, but it is far more fun to imagine that the woman is not the mother of this man's children or grandchildren. In any case, they clearly seem happy to be strolling along under the stars, and the kiss he plants on her lips suggests this is quite possibly not a father/daughter situation.

Needless to state, I did not engage this particular couple in conversation. I can only hope Nosy Nelly will stumble upon them for details of the relationship before the cruise is over. Since I still haven't seen Nell in quite a while, I have to assume that things must be going well with Seamus.

As your cruise progresses, you may observe guests eating by themselves and imagine how lonely they must be when in storms a person who joins them at the table with a litany of apologies for being late. Others will not be so lucky or unlucky, but the beauty of people-watching is that it allows the imagination to picture whatever it chooses. Years ago, I told my wife that a female acquaintance kept winking at me. She burst my bubble when she advised me that the woman had an astigmatism that caused her to wink at everyone. This was certainly less embarrassing than the time at home when I thought a woman was playing footsie with me under the dinner table, only to learn that the family dog was chewing on my sock.

While sitting poolside one afternoon reading a book, call me crazy, but I couldn't help but notice a lovely lady sitting across the pool in a smart-looking bikini. Hard as I tried not to stare, my attention kept drifting in her direction. It wasn't until Bruno tapped me on the shoulder and inquired about my particular interest in his girlfriend that I decided I'd spent enough time in the sun than I needed that day.

In this way, people-watching is the kind of sport you don't want to get caught participating in. You also have to accept that this sport is almost always a two-way game. Once, while docked in Shanghai on a cruise off the coast of China, I felt like I was being watched. Constantly.

Now, the Shanghai of thirty years ago was not as sophisticated as that seaport is today, and that visit to the linen factory was a highlight unto itself. Still, every time I touched a fabric, two or three women would touch it as I moved away. When my wife went to a different table, she found herself followed by an ever-increasing group of women. Finally, she settled on some linen table napkins and headed to the cashier to pay the bill. Instantaneous was the response. Every woman who had been watching was now standing in line with linen table napkins offered up for purchase.

Beijing, a three-hour drive inland from the port, would be our final destination before returning home from a marvelous vacation that had begun in Hong Kong. If we thought we'd been followed in Shanghai, we hadn't seen anything yet. The markets of Beijing in 1992 were just beginning to welcome westerners. This made us into an attraction all by ourselves whenever we ventured out from the hotel into the markets. Men and women, boys and girls, and locals of all ages watched everywhere we went and everything we touched. We were like the grand marshals of a parade through the streets of Beijing. It felt nice to bask in the limelight for a time, but we couldn't help but worry that the state's security personnel might have been among the watchers. Just in case, we stayed on our best behavior and avoided any possible confrontation with the police.

Pick almost any port in the world of cruise-ship travel, and you will find an opportunity to watch and be watched. Whether it is on the topless beach in Nice, France, or the line forming at the Louvre in Paris, you'll have no trouble encountering unusual sights. If you visit the American cemetery in Normandy, you can watch and shed a tear with fellow visitors. In Moscow, at the end of a river cruise, you may watch those coming and going through Red Square and the Kremlin, knowing that they may be watching you as well. If you're visiting St. Thomas on a Caribbean cruise, the diamond sellers will be watching your every move. In New Orleans, you can watch just about anything and everything your heart desires. In Ft. Lauderdale, you can watch your fellow passengers come aboard. Whenever you travel, you won't have to look very far at all for people to watch and by whom to be watched.

Part 3:

BOOKING YOUR BEST CRUISE

10
Now It's Your Turn

I HAVE TO admit that I harbored some apprehension about being one of the first to set out to sea on a mega cruise vessel when ports around the world began to reopen. Fortunately, it took very little time for me to realize how spectacularly the cruise industry had performed in making its ships and voyages safer, healthier, and even more wonderful than before the pandemic struck.

By the time I began writing Part 2, which sets the table for what you might expect in terms of accommodations, dining options, excursions in ports of call, and activities and entertainment aboard the vessel, I was in full-steam-ahead mode. I had a blast introducing you to my friend Doug, Energetic Eve and her husband Easygoing Eddie, Rose Dawson (a.k.a. Florence Reid), and even the Archie Bunker clone. I am hoping that Nosy (yet endearing) Nelly provided a laugh or two, if only at least a smile.

Now comes the true challenge—the big effort that will decide whether this book ultimately meets its goal of winning you over to the world my wife and I have come to love. Let's see if I can make things a bit easier for you as you decide upon and then book your cruise.

Every day, I receive a batch of emails inviting me to book a cruise with one or more travel agencies or direct from the various cruise companies. If you simply take the time to Google "ocean cruises" and hit send, you will soon begin receiving advertisements from a host of cruise-marketing companies informing you of where and when you might wish to go and how much it will cost you. This will allow you to gain information germane to the subject without having to leave your home or workspace. If you are willing to receive postal mail, you can provide just enough information to start receiving printed brochures in your mailbox on a regular basis.

Before long, you will have learned more than you might imagine about cruise vacation options available to you and those you wish to accompany you. Armed with this background information, you may confidently make an appointment with a local travel agency, where you can discuss your interest in booking a cruise. Or you could simply call a specialist from a nationwide cruise-marketing company and ask your questions over the phone.

For those who are not new to cruising, it's always a good idea to broaden your horizons by looking into ships and cruise lines you have not yet considered. You will remember that there are over three hundred ships to choose from, sailing under names and cruise lines too numerous to name. We tend to be creatures of habit, frequenting the same restaurant over and over again, never taking the time to appreciate the offerings at other establishments. The same may be said of selecting a ship or cruise line. My wife and I have often met people who book the same ship year after year after year. As frequent passengers, we have occasionally fallen into this category. By expanding our base, we have been able to experience the very diverse choices available to us, and we've never looked back with a single regret.

Before continuing on this journey with me, I recommend that you set this book down for a moment (or even longer), step away, take a deep breath, and immerse yourself in a bit of daydreaming. Whenever I plan my next cruise vacation, I will spend some time closing my eyes and imagining I'm in a place far away, looking over the side of the ship as it glides through the water en route to a port that has yet to be determined. Where I will next venture may be a place I have read about, viewed pictures of, or seen in a movie.

Today, I am imagining the ship docking in the tropical waters of French Polynesia, a place I have always imagined as both beautiful and serene, though I have never visited in person. Many people have told me that

I must make time to visit South Africa, spend a day or two in Cape Town, and then embark on a voyage that will include an African safari. Another benefit of this trip is that it then makes its way through Indonesia before ending in Singapore. If I'm facing any time or seasonal constraints, I sometimes think of revisiting the Caribbean, just to get away for a week or ten days.

Well, now that we've done our daydreaming, let's get back to the business at hand. Let's continue through the process of booking that first or next cruise. Until now, you have traveled vicariously through my eyes and words. The time has arrived for you to begin making decisions that meet your unique needs. In the remaining pages, I hope to guide you through the various stages of booking and enjoying a cruise of your design—a vacation so singular in its amazingness that it is sure to compel you to create your own scrapbook or photo album compiling the smile-inducing memories of the people you met and the places you have visited, memories you will carry with you for the rest of your life.

Hopefully, the pages to come will open your eyes to what type of cruise is best for you, where you might choose to visit, and who (if anyone) to bring along with you. I will point out the differences between a three-day cruise to nowhere, a seven-day island-hopping cruise, a fourteen-day trek across the ocean, the charm of river cruises, and sightseeing cruises to some of the most famous ports in the world. Along the way, I hope to spark your inspiration as you decide on where to go, for how long to cruise, on what size ship, and how best to book the trip once you have made your selection.

On that latter front, you will also find information on how to maximize your cruise by deciding whether to purchase beverage packages and/or cruise-arranged air travel. Further, you will learn about additional perks such as pre- and post-cruise overnight stays in the port city, free tour excursions, and included gratuities for the crewmembers. These perks are frequently offered when the ship is not booked to capacity or at times such as this when the cruise lines are attempting to win back our patronage.

So what are we waiting for? Let's get started.

Don't Skip the Travel Agent

As I mentioned earlier, there is a wealth of information available to help you make your dream a reality. Once you are armed with this information, I implore you to seek professional help before diving into the water. Travel agents and cruise consultants are professionals at what they offer, and they only get paid when you choose to book through them. It costs you nothing to book through a professional, as they are compensated by the cruise company, and not by you paying an extra fee. In fact, you may save money by utilizing their services, as they know how to find discounts and perks that you and I are not privy to.

My first piece of advice on this subject is to select a travel agent who is well respected in your locale. Ideally, he or she will be well versed in available cruises and has a fair amount of experience in this area of vacation travel. If you do not require face-to-face personal contact, you will find that the large nationwide companies which specialize in cruising are no further away than dialing an 800 number. Booking cruises is what they do, 24/7/365.

Utilizing a travel professional isn't just something I recommend for first-time cruisers. This advice applies to all of us, myself very much included. I may have booked and enjoyed over fifty cruises, but I have never and will never book without first consulting with my travel consultant, Morgan, who has become my friend over the years. I stumbled upon Morgan almost twelve years ago after my original travel agent retired. I dialed an 800 number, and by chance, wound up speaking to Morgan on the other end of the line.

Morgan was quick to learn as much as possible about me and my family make-up, what I did for a living, what my interests were, where we had traveled in the past, and what it was we were looking to enjoy in our cruise. I was so impressed with his knowledge of cruising, his willingness to learn as much as possible about me and my family, and his demeanor that I knew I had been fortunate to have him be the one to pick up the phone. As experienced as I was when I placed that call, I could see quickly that I needed his help in making my decision. Even veteran travelers will make a mistake now and then. Not everything we see and read in a brochure proves true to life. This is where professionals like Morgan earn their keep.

On that first call to Morgan, having taken as many as twenty cruises by then, I felt like I should be telling him what I wanted rather than the other way around. When I told him the name of the cruise line, the name of the ship, the itinerary I was contemplating, and the dates of travel, there was a noticeable pause before Morgan spoke.

"Are you familiar with the ship you're considering?" he asked.

"My only exposure is the online brochure."

"I ask because other customers have told me that this ship has gotten a little old looking. And they say the food and entertainment is subpar."

With this revelation, I let Morgan steer me in a different direction. It turned out that he had steered us well. The cruise we ultimately chose could not have been more perfect for our needs. As soon as we returned home, I called Morgan to tell him that we would be happy to let him guide us on all future bookings. To this day, I would never consider booking a cruise without Morgan's help.

As an important aside, he always seems to get me a better deal than I would be able to secure on my own. He invariably gets me a perk or two, often with an existing-customer discount, and he always throws in a bit of onboard credit to spend as I choose.

Actually, that reminds me ... It's time to start planning for my next few cruises before I'm left behind and out of opportunity.

A Time to Learn

I MIGHT BE getting slightly carried away here and stressing you out. Don't worry. The myriad choices available should not cause you stress. Rather, if you approach things with a clear and level head, having a wide range of options can help you make a good decision. As with everything in life, trial and error applies to vacation planning as well.

And in any case, since you will have read this book, you couldn't possibly make the kinds of mistakes made by some of the people who have called Morgan over the years. When I asked my longtime travel agent whether he has ever fielded any dumb questions or comments from would-be clients, he provided a veritable treasure trove.

"I have some favorites," he told me. "After booking a cabin with a private balcony, a woman suddenly turned panicky and asked, 'Is this cabin under water?'

"'No, ma'am,' I told her. 'If it were, opening the sliding door would cause a significant moisture problem.'

"She was fine with that explanation."

Morgan also shared the story of a client who absolutely had to know the color of the bathroom shower curtain in her stateroom because, "In those tiny bathrooms, the shower curtain will affect my makeup choices."

Another young man called in thinking about booking his first cruise, but he had one important question: Are cruise ships made from wood or fiberglass?

"Actually, these ships are made of steel," Morgan told him.

The young man replied with an expletive that implied he thought Morgan was a liar. "Steel don't float!" he insisted.

"Then there was the time I was on the line with a gentleman who wanted to book a seven-night cruise from New York to the Bahamas. He wanted me to ask the cruise line how much it would cost to have the ship stop and pick him up at the port in Philadelphia."

Of course there are always questions from the geographically challenged as well, like the potential customer who called asking for a two- or three-day cruise from New York City to Aruba with maybe a stop in Mexico or Jamaica. One of Morgan's coworkers once took a call from someone who wanted to know the price for a cruise from Los Angeles to Las Vegas. The caller assured him that he had friends who take these cruises all the time, so he should just give him the price already so he could book.

"Four trillion dollars," Morgan's coworker told him after a long, circular debate. "That's what it would take for the Army Corps of Engineers to dig a canal from Los Angeles to Las Vegas so you can take your cruise."

Finally, a Florida resident called in looking for a seven-night Alaska cruise. The only stipulations were that it had to travel round-trip from Miami, and the journey had to be completed within the first two weeks of February.

To be fair to these callers, even experienced cruisers like me will make a mistake sometimes. Pictures in brochures are just that—pictures. We have booked hotels that look fabulous online, only to find that the picture was nothing like the room or hotel we imagined. This is another reason to seek professional help. As frequent cruise participants, we have met many people cruising for the first time. More often than not, these first-timers are glad they took the plunge. Many are so glad that they already start planning their next cruise while aboard the first one.

Keep in mind also that your first cruise is bound to be as much a learning experience as it is an enjoyable one. The only way to know for certain what kinds of cruises you favor is to go on one (or several). If you booked an inside cabin because of price, you may realize that an upgrade to an outside stateroom with a balcony is worth the modest increase in cost for your next cruise. It won't take long for you to realize whether you prefer to sail with thousands of passengers on a large ship or opt for the intimacy of a smaller vessel. Within the first few meals, you will figure out if you prefer the buffet versus the sit-down meal in the dining room, the early rather than the later seating, or the option of anytime dining. You may even choose to reserve a table in a specialty restaurant on occasion. If you are looking for rest and relaxation and not wanting to leave the ship each day to tour a port, you may look at cruises with more sea days and fewer stops along the route.

You will also learn that not all ships are created equal, and while older ships offer charm, newer ships may include more recent innovations including rock climbing walls, four-story pool slides, and movies under the stars. Not all cruise lines are created equal either, and it should not surprise you that a cruise of the same duration with a similar itinerary may differ in price by many thousands of dollars depending on the cruise line you select. Only you will know your budget, but my advice is to spend a little more, if practicable, to maximize your enjoyment. Remember that this is a long-awaited vacation you're planning.

Don't be afraid to ask questions of your fellow passengers, as well. Once on board, if you so choose, you will meet plenty of people. Some of them may have accumulated thousands of sailing days over a period of years. These avid cruisers will gladly share their experiences with you if you open yourself to learning from them. You will likely come away with a wealth of knowledge to store for future planning. We all started as first-timers, and what I learned on that first cruise has proved valuable to me in planning the many cruises I have since enjoyed.

Broaden Your Horizons

OVER THE YEARS, my wife and I have visited much of the world, but I still have so much more I would love to see. We have been to every Caribbean island—some of them more than once. We have cruised to Alaska and included a land tour extension to gather an appreciation for that beautiful land and its native people. A cruise from South America enabled us to visit Antarctica. If you get a chance to go on such a trip, you will find the cleanest air and water in the world. We have traversed the Panama Canal and visited Mexico and Central America along the way.

On other cruises, we have been able to learn about distant places like New Zealand, Australia, and the countries of Asia to their north. We were fortunate to cruise the China Sea and enjoy Hong Kong for a few extra days. Europe is a place we love to visit, and a quick look at a map will awaken you to the number of ports Europe has to offer. There are many, nearly all of them worth the stop.

If you live in the United States or Canada, you don't even have to go very far from home, as cruises routinely traverse the east and west coasts of North America, from Florida to Montreal on the Atlantic side and from San Diego to Vancouver on the Pacific. You may also cruise to and from Hawaii from California, or you can fly and simply cruise the Hawaiian Islands for a week. Sooner or later, you may even embark on what has become our favorite cruise of all: a cross-ocean sail to or from Europe for fourteen days. We will often bookend this cruise with some time to explore the grand cities of Paris, Rome, Barcelona, Lisbon, and too many others to name.

Think Like an Infant

DECISIONS, DECISIONS, DECISIONS! If this is your first cruise, why not do what infants do? We all started out by crawling before we learned to walk. I suggest that you do the same by booking a cruise where you may join the ship after a short flight or drive to the port. A seven-day or even a five-day voyage should be sufficient to give you a feel for whether cruising is for you. There are many itineraries that fit the bill. I know many people who have done this, and it gave them a taste of what to expect on a longer journey, and also whether cruise vacations were something they would continue to pursue.

I do not recommend a three-day cruise to nowhere for your first cruise, as these are best referred to as party cruises which, while a lot of fun, will not be reflective of what true cruise vacationing has to offer.

If you decide to crawl before you walk/run, then over time, you will figure out what it is you wish to enjoy on your cruise vacation. If you are traveling with children, activities that keep their interest will be important. If you are traveling as a couple, your choices will be more or less unlimited depending on the amount of time you have available. If you are cruising as a single, you will only have to ask yourself what it is you are looking to accomplish. No matter what that may be, there is likely a cruise specialized to your wishes.

All in the Family

SPEAKING OF FAMILIES, we live in a family-oriented world, and that reality certainly extends to vacation planning. Whether it's during spring break from school, summer recess, or the year-end holidays, families like to pack up the kids and visit fun places. Cruising with the family is an option that has become very popular in recent years. The key to making the most of a family cruise vacation is picking the right cruise. And picking the right cruise is a matter of asking the right questions (first of yourself, and later, of your travel agent).

The most important question: do your children want to spend seven, ten, or fourteen days on a ship that sails the ocean with very few, if any, stops along the way?

If you have teenagers: are your teenage children going to enjoy being in close quarters with their parents and younger siblings for a week or longer?

If you have younger children: will there be enough for the preteen and younger age groups to keep them busy and not constantly under your feet and the feet of others?

Depending on how you answer these questions, different cruises will be better than others. Obviously, the word "Disney" suggests a product that is geared to families of all ages. Whether you are young or simply young at heart, Disney will offer a vacation that is certain to make every member of your family enjoy the experience. Make no mistake, however, as there are a number of other cruise lines that also offer family-oriented experiences, some of which are just as spectacular. Many of the newer ships sailing the seas offer activities that are certain to keep the kids busy while Mom and Dad, or Grandma and Grandpa, enjoy themselves as well. While the younger children are climbing a rock wall, sliding down that four-story pool slide, or surfing in the jet-propelled pool, the teenagers can keep busy in a specially designated area of the ship limited only to them and the things teens enjoy.

When evening rolls around, there will be movies shown for people of all ages. In one of the many lounges aboard, the kids may enjoy a magician performing while Mom and Dad enjoy a cocktail and the music of their era. Comedians usually adapt their material to the age preferences of their audience, and it is customary to provide late-night entertainment that will appeal to parents and their teenage children while the younger set is tucked in for the night.

Depending on the region of the world in which you are cruising, your entire family is certain to delight in the natural beauty of a glacier or a fjord as the ship passes by. Simply by looking over the side of the ship, family members may be able to spot whales, sea turtles, and dolphins swimming alongside the vessel.

When the ship docks in a port, the family may choose to join a snorkeling tour aboard a catamaran, a ride in a glass-bottomed boat, sign-up for a whale-watching cruise, or simply find a beach at which to sun and swim for the day. Not to be underestimated is the educational value of a visit to a historic site or a day of sightseeing in a city that the family has never before been fortunate to explore.

When considering traveling with family, it is also important to consider the size of your ship. The larger the ship, the more likely it is to offer activities and amenities for the family to enjoy. Larger ships will have multiple swimming venues, and at least one of the swimming pools will be geared to children or family activities. There will also be more variety of entertainment options on a large ship, which is likely to have an arcade for children of all ages to play the kinds of games found at carnivals and amusement parks.

For any children who love shopping, large cruise ships sometimes also feature a scaled-down version of a shopping mall. Dining venues ranging from a diner or ice cream parlor to a fast-food restaurant or hot-dog stand will make the family feel right at home.

In deciding what cruise is best suited to you and your family, you should take into account that your children will probably prefer to interact with other children in their age group. Teenage children likely want to meet and enjoy the company of other teens who are traveling with their own families. Teens rarely want to spend their vacation babysitting their younger siblings while Mom and Dad are out and about having a good time. Children of all ages won't want to be told to be quiet, stop running around, or avoid getting in the way of older passengers.

As a regular cruise vacationer who travels with my wife and not my family—who are by now grown and doing their own thing for vacations—we tend to look for a little less activity than the family-oriented cruise itineraries have to offer. When we book a cruise, we look to times of the year when the children are in school and not sailing alongside us. We also seek out cruises on smaller ships with longer itineraries, where families are not as likely to be on board.

Several cruise itineraries discourage family travel, as they choose not to equip these ships to entertain families and the amenities children require to enjoy their vacation. Although it is a rare occurrence, certain cruises will go so far as to clearly state that children cannot be accommodated.

We who are traveling without children should be equally careful in selecting the cruise that is right for us. Some passengers might prefer to be in the company of families, as it will make them feel young again. Many others will choose to seek out cruises where the entertainment and activities are more likely planned for an adult audience. Still others are looking for a sedentary experience, where very little structure is offered other than a good dining experience and an opportunity to seek out a quiet place to curl up with a book. Any couple traveling without family or friends should also take into account the make-up of the cruise passenger manifest.

A few years ago, my wife and I came within minutes of booking a cruise on a ship where we learned in the nick of time that we might be the only passengers who spoke English. The ship and itinerary seemed perfect for us until we learned that ninety percent of the passengers only spoke Italian. We would have been at a tremendous disadvantage to enjoy and understand what was going on around us.

Another example was the time we were thinking of booking a cruise on a smaller ship when we asked just enough questions to learn that eighty percent of the ship was booked by a group traveling together, which meant the cruise was likely to offer activities more geared to the group than to those of us who were just looking forward to a quiet getaway.

Cruising Solo

CRUISING ISN'T JUST for families or couples traveling alone. Sailing alongside you may be singles who have come aboard without a partner or companion. You may be surprised to learn that increasingly more passengers fall into this grouping than you might have imagined. It takes a lot of self-confidence to travel anywhere by yourself, but cruising actually is one of the easiest ways for a single to travel.

There will be activities that encourage those traveling alone to meet other singles, including "meet and greet" gatherings around the cocktail hour before dinner is served. When I crossed the Atlantic as a single some years ago, I mostly kept to myself, took many meals in my cabin, slept soundly, and was able to tackle some productive writing. Whenever I ventured out, I managed to meet interesting people.

Right on cue, just when I thought I'd lost contact with my friend Nelly, she popped up out of nowhere at a cocktail party for singles last night. If you are wondering what

I was doing at a singles get-together, the answer is that I viewed my participation as a research mission for this chapter of the book. My wife and I discussed my desire to attend, and we reached a compromise of sorts. She would not object so long as she could also attend—arriving alone, of course. As long as I was a good boy, we wouldn't have a problem.

It was then that I encountered Nelly and her friends Nancy and Marie, although they were pretending not to know each other.

"What are you doing here?" Nell snuck up behind me. "I thought you were a happily married man."

"I'm doing some research for the book." I pointed inconspicuously over my shoulder. "If you look over that way, you'll see my wife making sure that research is my only purpose for being here."

Nelly laughed, then donned a conspiratorial gaze.

"I should ask you the same question," I said. "Where's Seamus this evening?"

"Seamus had one too many glasses of Guinness after lunch. He's snoring away, I imagine, in his suite. I decided to see who else might be available for a dance or two after dinner. I'm on vacation, after all."

"Nancy and Marie are here, too, I see. Although you'd never guess you're traveling as a threesome."

"I told you we were able to take care of ourselves. Besides, we have a little bet on who gets asked to dinner first. I have to get moving or I'm going to come up on the short end."

As I continued to observe the growing number of men and women in attendance, I realized for the first time that it was true that many people do travel alone. It made me particularly happy to see a lady who resembled my dear acquaintance Florence Reid sitting at a table speaking with a gentleman who looked to be having a good time as the two of them enjoyed a glass of wine. The days of feeling sorry for people traveling alone were over for me, and it made me feel happy that cruising was and will always be for everyone and anyone.

My research completed, I headed for the exit, only to bump into Archie Bunker's double from the shore excursion. His wife was nowhere in sight. I couldn't resist asking him where his wife was and what he was doing at a singles' gathering, but before I could speak, he took the initiative.

"What's going on in here?" he growled at me. "I didn't see this advertised in the bulletin."

"It's a 'meet and greet' for passengers traveling alone," I explained. "What brings you here?"

"My wife told me to go for a walk. I think I was getting on her nerves. Maybe I'll just stop in for a beer or two and get the lay of the land."

"Have fun!" And off I went.

A Nursing Home at Sea

SEVERAL YEARS AGO, a friend called to advise me that his father had died. After extending my condolences, I asked when and where his burial service would take place. He informed me that his mother and father had been on a cruise, something they did three times a year, when his father's heart gave out. So his father's would be a burial at sea with the entire family in attendance on a cruise still to be scheduled.

While I marveled about the existence of a couple as enamored with cruising as my wife and me, what really struck me was the notion that my friend's father loved being at sea even after having crossed the Atlantic on a troop carrier to join the fight during World War II.

With his book, *The Greatest Generation*, Tom Brokaw provided the inspiration for this section, which I include in part to honor our parents and grandparents. My own dear mother was not only a member of that generation; she was also a cruise enthusiast who sailed at least once a year until she suffered a debilitating stroke that necessitated nursing home care for the last two years of her life. I remember how painful it was for me and my family to witness her failing health, but I could never appreciate what she must have felt in those last two years after having lived such a full and active life.

Soon after my mother passed away, my wife and I were cruising when we observed a woman being wheeled about the ship by another woman who might have been a sister, a friend, or perhaps a hired aide. The woman appeared to be about my mother's age. Every time I saw her, she had a smile on her face and seemed to be enjoying herself. During the day, she would take in some sun by the pool. In the evening, we would spot her in the theater enjoying a show. It was then that I began to explore the possibility of people living out the end of their life on a cruise ship and not a nursing home.

In today's world, the charge for a nursing home bed runs anywhere from $150,000 to more than $180,000 per year. I know this because a large portion of my law practice involves transitioning seniors from their homes or independent living arrangements and into skilled nursing facilities. Needless to say, nursing homes don't sail the seven seas, nor do they offer the amenities of a cruise ship. Could it be that a cruise ship, in certain cases, could serve as a viable or even preferable alternative?

Now, before we dive into that question, I should present a caveat: I am not suggesting that all or even most nursing home residents are physically or mentally capable of living aboard a ship. Some require too much medical care to warrant considering this kind of experience. But for those who are able to function even at a compromised level, it might be worth exploring.

If you are a senior citizen considering how to manage your twilight care, then consider this: for as little as $600 per person per week, you and your attendant could share a room for about $62,400 per year in an inside stateroom. You might even live in a balcony stateroom for double that price, or $124,800 per year, which you might notice is still $55,000 less than the nursing home.

But what about care? As it happens, on our last cruise before the COVID crisis, I met a lady who seemed to be traveling alone, and when I started up a conversation with her, I quickly discovered that she was a fount of information about this concept.

"Is it difficult to travel by yourself?" I asked.

"Oh, I'm not alone," she said. "I'm traveling with my ninety-years-young husband. We've been married sixty-five years."

She went on to explain that her husband was unable to be out and about, so he spent his time in the cabin watching television or sitting on the balcony listening to music. "He tends to nod off every once in a while, but mostly he enjoys this arrangement."

"Is it a burden taking care of him while you're on vacation?" I asked.

"Oh mercy, no. These cruises are as much for his enjoyment as mine. We have room service together for breakfast. Whenever I decide to go ashore at a port, our cabin steward periodically checks in on how my husband is doing."

"Does he mostly do room service then?"

"Not always. When I'm on the ship, I'll have lunch in the buffet and bring him a sandwich and some fruit. At dinner, sometimes we'll order from the menu of one of the specialty restaurants."

"Does he get out for any of the shows?"

"No, I will typically see those on my own. After he's settled into bed for the night, I'll head down to the theater to take in the stage show."

"What about medical care?"

"There's always a doctor and nurse on board. And anyway, I always pack enough medicine for a three-month cruise."

"Three months?" I asked, stunned.

"Oh yes, we go for at least a few months at a time. Then, when it's time to return home, he and I are energized enough to stay the course until our next cruise is scheduled to embark."

So there you have it. Even if your physical situation has you confined to your room, you can always lean on room service. There are a doctor and nurse on staff to help take care of your medical needs. Today, in a post-COVID world, there is a team of doctors and nurses on board. And with handicap-configured staterooms with roll-in showers available on all vessels, a cabin steward to provide for the needs of your room, and a cleaning and sanitizing service on a daily basis, there isn't a whole lot separating a nursing home from a cruise ship in terms of care.

Obviously, there will be challenges to overcome in order to accomplish this alternative, but these challenges are clearly not insurmountable. I can say this with authority because my people-watching habit has directed me to witness dozens of captain's toasts to a seventy-fifth wedding anniversary or a hundredth birthday celebration.

Once, while leaning on the port-side deck at the start of a seven-day cruise some years ago, I observed a Rolls Royce drive right up alongside the gangway. I was surprised, to say the least, that this was allowed, until I saw the driver open the doors of the car and assist a couple, clearly well up in years, to exit the vehicle. The gentleman, in his seersucker suit, bright yellow tie, and straw hat, was accompanied by his bride, dressed in a calf-length white dress, a mink stole over her shoulders, and a flowered hat perched delicately on her head. Each sported ivory-handled, gold-plated canes, which they leaned upon heavily in their efforts to amble up the gangway. The driver followed with four of the finest leather suitcases I have ever seen. Once aboard, cruise staff greeted the couple with the warm hugs and enthusiastic handshakes of old friends.

Obviously, these were not first-time cruisers.

Whether they drive a Rolls or a Chevy to the port, when seniors board a ship, they can't help but be noticed.

One sunny afternoon, a man in a baseball-style cap with the letters "USMC" emblazoned along the beak sat next to me on the starboard-side deck. I knew, of course, that USMC spelled the initials of the United States Marine Corps. What I didn't know, but would soon learn, was that this gentleman had landed on Omaha Beach the morning of the D-Day invasion of occupied France. Thousands of others joined him that day, but how many of those men, aside from him, had left a bride waiting at the altar one week prior because the young marine wasn't allowed to communicate with the outside world for fear of tipping off the enemy that the invasion was imminent?

This story has a happy ending, as the now not-so-young marine survived the war and, two years later, married the bride who had waited for his return—hopefully not by literally waiting at the altar.

As I mentioned back in chapter 4, cruises offer two settings for dinner in addition to the anytime dining options. If you had to guess which seating is preferred among the older generation—early dining at 5:30 p.m. or late dining at 8:00 p.m.—you might wonder why some early diners don't arrive at the restaurant until 7:00 p.m. to eat their meal. With tongue in cheek, I report that sometimes people oversleep their afternoon nap, others forget where the dining room is located on the ship, and others are still enjoying cocktail hour and don't feel any reason to rush to dinner.

Don't get me wrong, at twenty years younger than many of these passengers, I sometimes forget where I parked my car at the grocery store or where I left my car keys at home. I have even found myself looking for my sunglasses when they're sitting on top of my head. My wife and I are more likely to choose anytime dining or visit the buffet, but more often than not, it will be long before the clock strikes 7:00 p.m. Many seniors opt for the later sitting, enjoy the later stage show, and you may frequently find them dancing the night away, long after I am tucked in bed for the night.

As I contemplate putting this chapter to sleep, let me conclude by stating that the experiences I have enjoyed by meeting passengers old enough to be my parents are, for me, reason enough to book passage on a cruise. Our senior cruise-mates are never loud or rude. They most often have interesting tales to share. They tend to listen to what you have to say without interrupting, and for the most part, they blend in perfectly with the overall population. Here's one piece of advice, however: before you choose to sit next to a senior in the theater, keep in mind that, throughout the show, you are likely to hear, "Honey! What did he say?"

Finally, I must reiterate the key piece of advice from this chapter: whether traveling with family, as a couple, or even on your own, travel consultants are always a good reference to have, as they are best equipped to help you decide which ship and itinerary is best suited to you and yours. They can help you select the specific cruise to meet the very diverse needs you desire to have satisfied. Between their input and a little research, you should have everything you need to ensure a great cruise vacation experience for you and your family. And hey, even if it's not perfect the first time around, if you think of it as a learning experience—or in my case, as a research project—you're sure to pick up plenty of information to make the next cruise even better.

11
Eeny, Meeny, Miny, Moe

BEAR WITH ME for a minute and pretend you are a child once more. While we're in this frame of mind, let's consider the children's counting rhyme "Eeny, Meeny, Miny, Moe" to help you decide where you may wish to go on your first or next cruise vacation.

If you have a map of the world handy—if you don't, perhaps you could print one for the purposes of this exercise—you can pick up a sharp pencil, close your eyes, place the point of the pencil on your map, and let your hand wander. Once you feel like you've moved it enough, you can open your eyes and see where it settled. Chances are, you'll have landed on a spot where one of the three hundred or more cruise ships presently in service will either visit or pass by on their way to their next port. Yes, it's true; cruise ships travel to or near every possible place on the map you have in front of you.

Unless you are planning to cruise around the world for the better part of a year, you will want to narrow your search just a bit. This chapter will attempt to help you do just that. Cruises range in duration from three-day voyages all the way up to 180 days or longer. Some visit tropical climates while others venture to places more temperate and even downright frigid. Some will visit small islands, and others will visit well-known metropolitan areas. Some will be a cruise to nowhere, cruises which serve to offer you a quick sea voyage. Others will take you across one of the oceans on your map. Whatever you enjoy and wherever you wish to go, you are certain to find a cruise that suits your taste. All you have to do is search.

In my earliest days of testing the cruise-ship vacation option, I favored cruises of a seven-day duration. This decision was in part based on my desire to determine if cruising was something I wished to pursue, but it was also based on the amount of time I had available for vacationing. Over the years, I have cruised for as short a period as three days, and my longest cruise to date has lasted twenty-two. Sometime in the future, my wife and I hope to take a thirty-day cruise or longer. Of the fifty or more cruises we have taken, we have booked passage with no fewer than ten different cruise lines on forty different vessels. My goal is not to lead you in one direction or another, nor is it to sway you toward one particular cruise line or ship. Every ship on which we have sailed has offered us something a little different than the other ships we have enjoyed.

Where to Start?

IF THIS IS your very first cruise, you may want to consider something in the seven- to ten-day category, where you can arrive at the port of embarkation with a minimum of fuss. I suggest this because seven days should be enough time to get a feel for life aboard a ship. You will have ample time to explore the various dining rooms, enjoy a few ports of call, and get a taste of the entertainment on offer. You will also be able to determine how your body reacts to sleeping in a bed while the ship glides over the sea beneath you. In a week's time, you'll have learned enough about yourself, about your loved one(s), and about whether you would prefer a larger stateroom on a future journey. You'll also figure out if you're the kind of person who can relax on this type of vacation.

You might notice that I didn't recommend the three- or four-day cruise for first timers. This might seem counterintuitive, because after all, if you've never cruised before, wouldn't it be better to dip your toes in the water rather than dive straight in? You might think so, but the problem with shorter cruises is that their duration simply isn't long enough for you to get the feel for life at sea. Short cruises, as I already mentioned, are typically party cruises, and while everyone likes a party, this type of cruise is quite different from what you would normally experience on a week-or-longer cruise. My suggestion is to save the three-day cruise for a getaway weekend or a break from an extended vacation you are enjoying in or near a port city.

Many first-time guests select a seven-day voyage from south Florida to the Caribbean and back because a short plane ride or even a car trip will get you to the port without having to cross an ocean to begin your cruise. The seven- or ten-day Caribbean cruises are so popular, in fact, that they depart the coast of Florida on an almost daily basis from November through April. Even in the off-season, these cruises remain on offer, though typically at a less-than-weekly rate of departure. They will visit four or five ports and still offer a couple of days at sea, which will give you the feel for the overall cruise experience.

Seven-day cruises are also offered from the west coast of the United States or Canada to Alaska. They appear on many bucket lists because so many people desire to view the beauty of the Alaskan glaciers at least once in their lifetime. Due to weather concerns, the Alaskan cruises are offered between May and September. If you turn this into a ten-day cruise, you will be able to sail to Alaska and back without having to fly home from a different port. Many people choose to add a four- or five-day land trip to an Alaskan cruise and enjoy the magnificent wilderness and wildlife that trips starting in Fairbanks have to offer.

Without having to leave the United States, you may also find cruises that hug the west and east coasts, some that sail between San Diego and Seattle, with stops in Los Angeles and San Francisco; and some that head north from Ft. Lauderdale to Boston, with ports of call in Charleston, South Carolina, New York City, and Bar Harbor, Maine. You may also include ports in Canada if, on the west coast, you select a voyage that begins or ends in Vancouver; or, on the east coast, a cruise that originates or terminates in Montreal.

Also available and extremely popular are cruises that visit the Hawaiian Islands. For these cruises, you will have the option of flying to and from Hawaii and then embarking on a seven-day voyage that will make calls on four or five of the islands and give you the chance to get a feel for the unique nature of each island. On these cruises, you have the opportunity to see an active volcano, visit a rainforest, and enjoy the beauty of the beach at Waikiki, all very different experiences on three separate islands. Another enjoyable way to visit Hawaii is to sail for six days from San Diego, spend five days touring the Hawaiian Islands, and then retrace your steps on a six-day cruise across the incredible Pacific Ocean. Not everyone has the eighteen days it takes to choose this option, but having done it both ways, I can state that both are worthy of your consideration.

What About Outside the U.S.?

MANY OF YOU will at some point select all of the voyages I have just described, enjoy them thoroughly, and never have to leave the good old USA. For others, you will look at that world map sitting on the dining room table and wonder what else there is to explore in this planet on which we live. If you are a cruise enthusiast like me, you will probably consider crossing an ocean either by plane or ship so you can see what you're missing in other countries.

My wife and I have flown to Europe, for instance, where we enjoyed seeing how people live in the various countries which comprise that continent and where we have boarded cruises of various types. We have gone from Amsterdam in the north, along the coast of France, with stops in Normandy and later in Bordeaux; we have also cruised to Lisbon and Barcelona, ending our cruise in Italy after getting a taste of Mediterranean Sea air and the different types of food these countries have to offer. On other trips, we have started in Rome, traveled south through Sicily, Malta, and Crete, and then headed north through the Adriatic Sea with stops in Dubrovnik and Split, Croatia, before leaving the ship in Venice.

In that same region of the world, you may take seven or ten days to see the Greek Islands of Mykonos and Santorini while also visiting Athens and Istanbul. You may choose to head further east through the Suez Canal and visit Israel and other stops in the Middle East, taking a look at the pyramids of Egypt before venturing further on to India and the Taj Mahal.

Do you want to see the United Kingdom without having to pack up and travel by train, plane, and ferry? Maybe you will want to consider a ten- or twelve-day cruise that begins in Southampton, England, and circles the U.K. with stops in Cork and Belfast, Ireland. You'll want to take a stop when you get to the hometown of the Beatles in Liverpool, England, before heading farther north to Glasgow and Edinburgh, Scotland, where you can find some of the great castles of the world. Completing the circle would be a sea day or two through the North Sea as the ship returns to Southampton, from which you might choose to then spend a few days in London before flying home.

In this part of Europe, also awaiting you is the Baltic Sea. Here, you can sail and visit Copenhagen, Denmark; Oslo, Norway; Stockholm, Sweden; Helsinki, Finland; St. Petersburg, Russia; Berlin, Germany; and Gdansk, Poland, all without ever having to repack your suitcase and hustle to catch a plane or train. When you return home from any of these historic and cultural centers, you might find yourself contemplating a return visit to spend more time in each location. It's this same sort of bug that has my wife and me adding more cruises to our agenda multiple times a year. We just can't get enough of seeing the world.

Before leaving Europe, I would be remiss if I didn't mention what's known in the cruise world as "repositioning" cruises. Each spring, cruise lines move a number of their ships from the east coast of the United States across the Atlantic Ocean to a host of ports in Europe, where they will spend the summer months cruising from port to port and giving you a chance to see some of the great cities of Europe.

These same ships reposition again in October and November, heading back to the U.S. They have become extremely popular to those of us who prefer extended days at sea. Although it only takes seven days to cross the Atlantic, these voyages tend to offer fourteen- or fifteen-day itineraries as they slowly cross the ocean with occasional visits to Bermuda and other islands situated in the Atlantic. The ship may visit the Canary Islands, Madeira, which is a Portuguese island, and even Gibraltar or the northern coast of Africa at Morocco. If time doesn't permit a fourteen-day journey, you may choose to sail on the Queen Mary II between New York and Southampton for seven days in either direction. This trip launches during most of the months of the year. If down-time is what you need, with a chance to read a book or two while enjoying wonderful food and drink, these repositioning cruises may be exactly what the doctor ordered.

But My Pencil Landed in the Southern Hemisphere...

HERE'S THE GOOD NEWS: we've only covered about a quarter of the world in which the cruise industry sails. Next, we head south to Mexico, Central America, and on to South America and even Antarctica.

If you are interested in cruising through the Panama Canal—which is, in my humble opinion, one of the greatest accomplishments of human ingenuity in history—you may do so from either coast of the United States, or even by originating your cruise from South America. Along your voyage, you will visit towns and villages in Central America and Mexico and stop along the Mexican Riviera. If you simply want to take the long route from the Atlantic to the Pacific, you may begin your cruise in Rio de Janeiro or Buenos Aires and sail south through the Falkland Islands on your way around Cape Horn to Santiago, Chile, or Lima, Peru. If you are fortunate to have the time, some of these cruises will also cross the Drake Channel and bring you through ice fields to the coast of Antarctica.

Summer in Antarctica begins in December, when the temperature actually reaches slightly above 32 degrees Fahrenheit. This is the only time of year you will be able to view the natural beauty of this lost continent, where you will breathe the cleanest air on Earth and view incredible ice formations rising from the sea before your eyes. Not to be ignored are the Chilean fjords, which compare favorably to the fjords of Norway and New Zealand, a place we will visit directly.

Are you up for a long flight? If the answer is yes, you will not want to miss the chance to visit Australia and New Zealand. Among our all-time favorites was the cruise we took from Auckland, New Zealand, along the coast through Tauranga, Queenstown, and Christchurch, New Zealand, then farther south to the Australian island state of Tasmania, before heading north to Melbourne and ending in Sydney. It was, without a doubt, one of the most beautiful cruises we have ever enjoyed.

It is easy to understand why so many people, no matter what their country or background, fall in love with Australia and New Zealand. Some promise to return and retire there while others return to begin second careers. I suppose some would wish to stay if for no other reason than to avoid the long flight home. While it is possible to cruise all the way from the Americas to New Zealand and Australia, it will take a bit longer than a few weeks of vacation. If you live in the U.S., South America, or Europe, is it worth the long journey to see these countries firsthand? The answer is definitely yes, if only once in your lifetime. As you sail into Sydney and first lay eyes on the harbor and the Opera House, you will understand the appeal.

We might technically be crossing the equator again, but let's move a bit north on our journey, shall we?

There are so many different cruise itineraries covering these regions that it would prove difficult to enumerate all of them in this chapter. Suffice to say, you may fly to Singapore, board a cruise ship, and set sail in one of four different directions. A popular itinerary will take you east to Bangkok, Thailand, Vietnam, Hong Kong, the coast of China with a stop in Shanghai, an inland trip to Beijing, and end in Tokyo, Japan.

Almost thirty years ago, my wife and I flew to Bangkok, spent three nights there, then flew to Hong Kong, where we enjoyed another three nights before boarding our ship for a ten-day voyage along the Chinese coast and up the Yangtze River. I am certain that I would not recognize the Shanghai and Beijing of today, and when I look at pictures of those two cities, I ask myself where those high-rise buildings came from. The civil turmoil in Hong Kong wasn't present in those days, and what I remember of that wonderful visit may be more difficult to replicate today.

All this, and we still haven't visited the continent of Africa, save for stops in Morocco and Egypt. If you think fifty cruise vacations is a large number, then how is it that my wife and I have yet to visit Cape Town, South Africa? Or cruise the African coast while day-stopping in Richards Bay for a taste of a safari?

Or how come we have yet to explore Singapore or Tokyo and the many islands of Indonesia? Do I have enough years left to cruise to French Polynesia, or to see it all on a 180-day cruise around the world?

I can only hope so. And come to think of it, these are just stops in locales that border an ocean or sea. What if your pencil landed somewhere further inland? Well, have I got some good news for you...

The Charm of River Cruising

I HAVE BEEN asked time and again—mostly by family and friends who know I'm writing a book encouraging people to consider taking a cruise vacation in the post-COVID era—if I'm considering writing a segment that speaks to the charm of river cruising. Given the fact that my river-cruising experiences are somewhat limited when compared to the number of ocean voyages we have booked and completed, I was a bit reticent about attempting to portray myself as a seasoned veteran of the river-cruise world. Of the fifty-plus cruises we have taken, only five have come aboard vessels that sail rivers and not oceans, unless you include one small ocean-going ship that focused its itinerary on various rivers in Europe. It was only after my editors echoed the sentiments of my family and friends that I succumbed to the challenge of writing this piece.

First, the obvious: river cruises are so different from ocean cruises that the subject actually warrants a book of its own. In the words that follow, I will give my best effort at doing justice to a form of cruising that is worthy of your consideration when next you contemplate a vacation at sea. The first thing I ask you to do as you read this section, however, is to put blinders on and not envision a vessel the length of three football fields standing as many as fourteen or fifteen stories tall above the water. The ship you are contemplating when booking a river cruise will likely be a touch shorter in length than one football field and will have only two or three decks visible. Instead of traveling with as many as one thousand, two thousand, three thousand, or even six thousand other passengers, your river ship will have a capacity of between 130 and 190 guests. If that doesn't sufficiently describe the river-cruise ship, take note of the fact that the vessel will be about the same width as the swimming pool on an oceangoing ship. I relate these facts not to deter you, but rather to inform you that much of the charm of a river cruise is its intimacy.

From the moment you board your river ship, you will begin to understand the not-so-subtle differences between river and ocean cruising. Instead of climbing a gangway, you may only have to cross through two or three other river-cruise ships that are moored to each other at the port. Where touring your ocean cruise ship requires two or more hours, you may be able to take in the amenities of your river ship in thirty or forty minutes. Your cabin may not be as large or opulent as on an oceangoing cruise, but in the world of river cruising, these are plusses and in no way negative features. River cruising has become popular—in fact, very popular—to the point of being able to compete for business with the mega-cruise industry.

Your river vessel might look more like a barge because of its length and tapered lines, but once aboard, you will enjoy visiting the restaurant and feel more at home than on the larger ships that sail the ocean. The lounge will be far smaller, but it will have ample room to accommodate the number of passengers with whom you will be sailing. There isn't likely to be a swimming pool on board, but there will be a lovely open area on the top deck to relax and soak in some sunshine during the day and appreciate the moon and the stars at night. When you wish to enjoy a cocktail, you won't have difficulty finding a seat at the bar. You will also enjoy the opportunity to have a quiet conversation with your companions in a not-so-noisy lounge. Entertainment will be on a more relaxed and smaller scale, but you are likely to be pleasantly surprised at its quality.

When your ship departs the dock en route to your first port of call, you might enjoy the comparatively gentle feeling of gliding on top of a river without the motion of the open sea. While walking around the vessel, you may see a bicycle rack from which you may select a bike to explore the area where next you will be visiting. Land will almost never be out of view. You will get a closeup view of castles and other beautiful structures, some of which will be hundreds of years old.

When navigating from port to port, the average speed of your river ship will be in the range of six knots per hour, or just under seven miles per hour, compared to the average speed of the ocean liner that will be traveling at seventeen knots, or approximately twenty miles per hour. This, too, adds to the intimate nature of the journey, as you will have time to set your camera sights on an object you are passing and take several photos or a video of the scene.

Although not all rivers are shallow, when the captain desires to bring the ship close to land or even through a narrow passageway, the draft of the river ship will allow for this without fear of running aground. It is quite common for river cruises to include very rustic villages in their itineraries, and guests will be given an opportunity to see up-close how these villagers live and work. If time allows, you may be invited into a home or two along the way to share some food or drink with your hosts.

As a novice to river cruising, I attempt not to overstate facts, but I speak with confidence and firsthand knowledge when I write that river ships will arrive at docks that most ocean vessels have no ability to navigate. This statement leads me to the ultimate charm a river cruise will offer: how would you like to wake up one morning on your cruise, open your curtains, and be looking at the

Eiffel Tower from a stone's throw away? Yes! When you cruise along the River Seine in the middle of France, in the city of Paris, you will have an opportunity to view Notre Dame Cathedral, the Louvre, and many other historical sites. You will also be able to sight-see Paris, and if you wish, you may choose to spend a night or two in the City of Light before or at the end of your cruise.

Seine River Cruises begin and end in Paris. They travel north to La Rouche and Rouen and spend a couple of days allowing tours of the Normandy beaches before heading downriver and returning to Paris. Other French river cruises include visits through wine country beginning and ending in Bordeaux, with visits to St. Emilion, Pauillac, Cadillac, and the Gironde Estuary. On this journey, you will tour wineries and vineyards and sample delicious wines of the region. You may also river-cruise in southern France and make ports of call in Lyon, Provence, Viviers, Avignon, and Arles as you approach the Mediterranean Sea. Every one of these towns and cities has something of interest to offer which will add to the overall enjoyment of your cruise. I have been fortunate to visit every one of these port cities in France, but only Bordeaux on a ship through the Gironde Estuary.

Next, how about we discuss a pair of journeys that my wife and I did make by river cruise? The first traveled along the Danube River, while the other cruised the rivers of Russia. These two journeys rank very high on our list of favorite cruises, and you will soon understand why that is so.

In December 2012, my wife and I flew to Budapest and joined a river cruise heading north along the Danube, which is sometimes referred to as "The Blue Danube" even though it happens to be brown. It is beautiful nonetheless. After spending two days enjoying both Buda and Pest, we arrived in Bratislava, Slovakia, a lovely town which has retained its Middle Age charm and character.

On Christmas morning, as already mentioned, we docked in Vienna, Austria, toured the city, attended Mass at the Cathedral, visited a beautiful palace, and attended a classical music concert. The next day proved equally special, as we visited Salzburg, Austria, a short drive from the river. Aside from serving as the location for "The Sound of Music," Salzburg is a city rich in history, architecture, and culture.

From there, we headed closer to Germany and made stops in Krems and Linz before leaving the ship in Passau. From Passau, we boarded a van which drove us through the Black Forest of Germany on our way to the city of Prague in the Czech Republic. We passed checkpoints that previously separated East from West Germany and arrived in Prague for a three-night visit that included New Year's Eve and Day. Incidentally, if this book fails to convince you of the joys of cruising and you never take a cruise of any kind, do be certain to add Prague to your list of must-visit places either way. It ranks right up there with Paris, London, and Moscow.

Speaking of Moscow, recently we booked a Russian river cruise which began in St. Petersburg and ended in Moscow. After three days and nights touring the palaces of Peter the Great, Catherine the Great, and the Hermitage Museum, we headed south along some of the cleanest and most beautiful waterways anywhere in the world. We made day-stops in Kizhi, Mandrogy, Kuzima, Yaroslavl, and Uglich on our way to Moscow. The history lessons learned along the route and the pleasure of meeting Russian people, who are among the friendliest we have encountered, would alone have made this voyage worthwhile. But Moscow is a city never to be taken for granted.

When you ride the subway system of Moscow, you will feel as though you are touring a museum of art and history. When you visit the Kremlin and Red Square, you'll be amazed at how even after the overthrow of the Czar, Russia's culture has been preserved and restored. Within the Kremlin itself, you'll find no fewer than five cathedrals dating to the seventeenth century in which there are more icons and murals of Christianity and Christ himself than you will find in the Vatican in Rome. When asked how these wonderful domes and churches survived the Bolshevik Revolution, native Russians will tell you that the Bolsheviks weren't savages, but merely socialists who wanted everyone to enjoy what had been previously reserved for royalty.

If you take a little time to research the world of river cruising, you will learn that similar voyages take place in other parts of Europe on rivers like the Rhone, the Rhine, and the Elba, and in countries all around the world. You may river cruise in China, Vietnam, Egypt, and Africa. If you choose to visit the interior portions of South America, you may wish to book a cruise that navigates the Amazon River for a week. While I am certain that these adventures are extremely worth the trip, I have not yet taken cruises of this type, so I will leave the subject to a different author.

In the U.S., Mississippi River cruises are quite popular. I have slightly more experience with this kind of cruise. On a paddle-wheel boat from New Orleans to Natches and Vicksburg, Mississippi, with stops in Baton Rouge and St. Francisville, Louisiana, along the Mississippi River, my wife and I feasted on oysters, gumbo, and jambalaya while tasting a bit of bourbon and a mint julep or two. The Southern hospitality was second to none, and the accommodations on board, while not modern in décor, made us feel as though we had rented a bedroom in a Southern mansion. Until you have watched the paddlewheel propel the ship from a nineteenth-century steam engine on a Mississippi riverboat, you have not experienced the history of the good old United States of America.

River cruising in the U.S. is also offered in the Pacific northwest along the Columbia and Snake Rivers between Portland, Oregon, and Clarkston, Washington, and also in the northeast in New England between Boston, Massachusetts, and Nova Scotia, Canada, with stops along the coastal waters of Maine in Portland, Bar Harbor, and Kennebunkport. In the midsection of the United States, you'll be able to cruise the Ohio River to the Mississippi River, beginning your voyage in Pittsburgh, Pennsylvania, while traveling through Marietta and Cincinnati, Ohio, then Louisville, Henderson, and Paducah, Kentucky on route to St. Louis, Missouri.

You know what's interesting? I was at first reticent to write a section on river cruises, given my comparatively novice experience with the subject. But now that I'm through writing about it, I find myself compelled to book at least a few more river cruises while I'm able. River cruising is clearly a relaxing way to enjoy your vacation on the water while others do the work. In the end, the charm of river cruising isn't the ship itself, but rather, where the ship takes you. If you want to visit the nooks and crannies of our world and see them from a different angle, then a river cruise is very much for you.

September Morn

I TEND TO get a little nostalgic from time to time. Whenever this mood strikes, I find myself humming the words of songs some of my favorite entertainers made famous in days gone by.

One notable time the mood struck me was the middle of September of that year we will never forget, when COVID-19 brought our world to a standstill. I happened to be on my way to work that crisp fall morning, the weatherman on the radio informing that it would be a beautiful afternoon with temperatures rising to the low 70s. Out of the clear blue, I found myself humming the song "September Morn," one of my favorite songs by Neil Diamond.

"We traveled halfway round the world," I sang to myself, "to find ourselves again, September morn."

I don't know about you, but back in September, as we were all in the thick of the second wave of the pandemic, I had fallen deep into cabin fever. Mentally, though not physically, I had taken a couple of cruises since the crisis began. When that song passed through my head that day, it compelled me to do something I had not yet considered: to book an actual, real-life cruise.

The year 2020 will be remembered for many different things, but none more than the disruption to life that the COVID pandemic has inflicted on our world. It is time to put this behind us and begin to live our lives fully, wiser nonetheless of ways to protect ourselves and those we love.

Just as people began traveling on airplanes after 9/11/2001, you and I may now return to doing the things that fulfill us. We can step out into a safer and cleaner world, all because of the processes introduced to protect us from forces beyond our control. My wife and I wasted little time getting back to doing what we love to do. As a result, I have been able to recount for you how wonderful that first post-COVID cruise was for us and the fellow passengers who joined us.

By now, assuming this book has met its goal, you are feeling reassured that a cruise vacation in a post COVID-19 world is safer than ever before. Hopefully, you have a better sense of what to expect once aboard. And in any case, you've certainly met some interesting people and have visited some exciting places. This is all good and well, but we have a key problem. So far, you've done all this only through the eyes and words of a third party, yours truly.

The time has come for you to decide if you're going to experience the world of cruising for yourself. The time has come to take the steps necessary to make this vacation a reality for you.

12
I've Made My Decision

AS WE NEAR the finish line, I honestly don't know what more I can write to help you make a decision to join me on a future cruise. Perhaps I could do what brochure producers do and insert photos of beautiful couples having a drink in one of the lounges of the ship they're advertising. Or maybe a picture of a butler serving dinner in a suite would do the trick. If I was enticing a family to commit, I might include a photo of a four-story pool slide.

As previously reported, I do not receive compensation from cruise lines or the travel industry for writing this book. What I have written comes from the heart. It is derived exclusively from personal experience, with a few minor flourishes to enhance the storytelling. On that latter point, I must confess that Nosy Nelly's name was not in fact Nelly. Or "Nosy," for that matter. She also underwent a bit of an evolution as a mostly-true-to-life character during the drafting of this book. In my first draft, she was more like an annoying obstacle than an overeager collaborator. I really did meet a woman precisely like her during a recent cruise, but for obvious reasons, my initial impression of her during that 5:00 a.m. meeting was less receptive. I am a morning person, but certain times of day are usually better for intrusions. In any case, my desire to write nice things about her only grew over time.

If the previous chapters have captivated you to the point of taking the next crucial step by booking a cruise, I'm glad to have been a part of that decision. In fact, as I near retirement, I intend to sail even more regularly than the three times per year my present schedule allows, and I would be thrilled to possibly meet you aboard a ship and learn that I played some small part in helping you make this decision.

If you aren't quite ready to book a cruise, the mere fact that you have stayed with me through these chapters tells me that your mind is still open to the possibility of taking a cruise vacation in the future. I hope this is true. As I look back over forty years ago to my first cruise, I must admit I had no idea that this form of vacation would become so important in my life. I remember going on that first cruise simply because good clients of my firm more or less insisted we join them.

Enough, then, about me. It's your turn to finish this book by making a decision: Do I, or don't I? Should we, or shouldn't we? Only you are capable of answering these questions. But if you're still on the fence, I'll make one last attempt to help...

Frank Sinatra, the same man who launched the career of the singer you met in chapter 6, knew how to get our attention when he bellowed out the tune "Come Fly With Me," a song that invited us to see and live the magic that worldwide travel could unveil. Now I invite you to "Come Cruise With Me" by walking up the gangway to board one of the three hundred or more luxury liners that sail our oceans and seas and experience firsthand the pleasures that await you on this now safer and healthier mode of travel vacation.

I can't be certain, but I think you might enjoy meeting a Nosy Nelly of your own. You might even ask a couple who resemble my friends Doug and Cathy to join you on your cruise. Sure, you will observe from time to time an Easygoing Eddie and Energetic Eve, and probably an Archie Bunker or two, but these are the encounters that will make you laugh when you're in the privacy of your cabin or stateroom. You won't want to miss the quality of entertainers like my Rosemary Clooney double, and I promise you that you'll seek out and perhaps fall in love with at least one Rose Dawson—excuse me, Ms. Florence Reid—before your cruise is over.

If, as I hope, you are truly ready to set sail, be sure to seek the help of a travel agent or cruise consultant. My decision to contact Morgan out of the clear blue more than twenty years ago has proven invaluable. Today, I view him as a friend as well as an adviser. He lives and works more than a thousand miles from my home, but we took the time a few years ago to meet in person and I also had the opportunity to meet his family.

As a parting gift for having stayed with me along this journey through the world of cruise travel, I wish to offer you a few tidbits of information to make you appear as experienced as I have become in booking a cruise. The word "perk" is a shortened version of the word "perquisite." The definition of the word is "an addition to something or an extra to a known condition." In the cruise world, a perk is something offered by the cruise line to help close a deal—or in this case, a booking.

As we emerge from the COVID pandemic, cruise companies are offering many such perks, including four category upgrades to the stateroom you would otherwise select. Other perks may include free excursions, all-inclusive bar packages, or round-trip airfare from home to the port. They may also include free gratuities, reservations in the specialty dining rooms with no upcharge, and one only can imagine what else. Reduced fares also tend to be a selling point. No matter the perk or perks being offered, always be aware that some of them may already be factored into the price of the cruise.

In the real-estate world, we hear terms like "buyer's market." I believe now is the time to take advantage of a buyer's market in booking a cruise. As cruise companies strive to return to sea with passengers and not just crew, the wise consumer is likely to find savings not otherwise available in prosperous times. Now may be just the right time to take advantage of this situation. One word of warning is offered: cruise enthusiasts like me are already learning that many people are itching to get back to sea, and that future cruises are beginning to see a rise in sales volume. Once the demand for staterooms reaches pre-COVID levels, I believe we'll see a reduction in the number of perks being offered. So in other words, if you want a deal, now is the time to take advantage.

That said, it's important to keep in mind that cruise companies are in the business of making a profit for their shareholders. They are also attempting to recover from a very expensive year of unexpected costs with no revenue to offset these costs. Some of the bargains being presented may already be factored into the bottom-line price we're being charged. Consider the all-inclusive bar package. You might have heard that in the food-service industry, the profit a restaurant makes is more likely to come from the sale of alcoholic beverages than the food. When a cruise company includes the bar package or unlimited beverage consumption in the price of the cruise, it is doing so with full knowledge that unless it factors this profit potential into the bottom-line price we pay, it's essentially giving away its most easily attained profit center. As such, it is better to ask a lot of questions about what you're actually receiving when this perk is presented. There is plenty to consider when determining whether it is worth accepting such an offer.

Free excursions are also something you might do well to discuss with a booking agent. I know from experience that it costs the cruise line a lot of money to place passengers on a bus and transport them to a site where an admission charge must be paid. All you need to understand is the price charged for an excursion when it is not included in the fare to realize that the perk has to be recovered somehow. The same is true for the cost of round-trip airfare and transfers to and from the ship and an airport.

On the other side of the coin, free dining in a specialty dining restaurant might actually be a true perk, as it will cost the company little to nothing to offer and may actually help the company ensure the social distancing of passengers.

The four-category upgrade, meanwhile, is not going to get you moved from a basic cabin to a luxury suite. It may well allow you to stay in a similar room but in a more preferred area of the ship. Your cabin may be upgraded from the front or back of the vessel to midship, and it may even cause you to be upgraded to a more preferable deck.

Worthy of a bit more discussion is the subject of gratuities. Prepaid gratuities means that at the end of your cruise, you won't be charged on your credit card for the cost of thanking crew members who have served you so well. If gratuities are not prepaid, either as a perk or in the bottom-line cost of your cruise, you will be charged between $13 and $16 per person, per day, of the duration of your cruise as a gratuity to be hopefully passed on to the crew and staff. This is no small amount when you compute it on your calculator.

I have been cruising for so many years that I remember well the days when my wife and I would secure a handful of envelopes from the purser's office. We would write personal notes to our cabin steward, his assistant, our waiter, his assistant, and our favorite bartender. Those notes would go into the envelopes with what we believed to be an appropriate amount of cash. Then we would hand-deliver those envelopes with a hug and a word of thanks.

The policy change to automatically add gratuities to everyone's final bill surely benefits all crew members. Some passengers used to avoid tipping altogether and would get away with it Scot-free. Even since the change, I have spotted certain passengers at the purser's office on the final night of a cruise asking to have the gratuities removed from their account on the premise that they have paid for service in their own fashion. Only they will know the truth of that claim. It's good that the lovely, hardworking people aboard every cruise ship don't have to worry so much about that anymore. But at the same time, I will miss the personal interaction that the envelope system provided.

The Final Words

IN THE MOVIE "Patton," shortly after his titular character hands Field Marshall Erwin Rommel's panzer brigade a stunning defeat by laying wait in a well-concealed defensive position, George C. Scott utters the words, "Rommel, you genius! I read your book."

I don't claim to be a genius, but when I see you on the high seas in the near future, I would be honored to hear you say, "Greg, I read your book, and that's one of the reasons I'm here on this cruise."

Stay safe! Stay healthy! And have fun at whatever you choose to do in life.

Epilogue

MY UNDERSTANDING OF an epilogue is that it is meant to advise the reader about what happened to certain characters after the conclusion to the story. For instance, a character who barely survived an attack at the end of a novel makes a miraculous recovery in the epilogue and goes on to live an accomplished life. In this book, the epilogue is intended to let you meet a few of the true-to-life people I met on my first post-COVID cruise. It should come as no surprise that many of the characters you met in this book are either entirely fictitious, an amalgamation of multiple people from real life, and in the case of my friend Doug, as real as life its own self. Now I want you to meet a few people whom, if you are lucky, you may actually get to meet on your first or next cruise.

Let's begin with Dawn and Dennis. We met this couple at a captain's meet and greet and soon learned that Dennis was a retired Air Force officer who flew an assortment of planes dating back to the Vietnam era, where he saw combat duty. Dennis was reticent to speak about those early days but couldn't wait to regale us with stories about his wife Dawn, also an Air Force officer. It seems that the military sent Dawn to law school, which began a career prosecuting and defending Court Martial trials until she was appointed a military judge deciding cases in Iraq, Afghanistan, and Europe. As her career advanced, Dawn became Chief Judge of the Air Force in Europe and eventually Chief Judge of the entire United States Air Force. The time spent with this lovely couple was a highlight of the cruise.

Meeting Brendan and Chris was a little like meeting Easygoing Eddie and Energetic Eve from the book. I met Brendan sitting poolside with a drink and a cigarette in hand. He looked a little like Santa Claus, and when I overheard his healthy laugh, I stopped to say hello. He was full of stories from his years as the operations officer for Air Lingus at JFK airport in New York. Brendan was settled in for the afternoon when his best friend Chris, who had invited him on the cruise after receiving a one-week pass from his wife, arrived to see what the rest of the day had in store. Chris, a successful businessman from New Jersey, was not one to sit around for a long period of time, always on the move to his next activity. This gave me an opportunity to seek out Brendan and enjoy his stories every afternoon, knowing exactly where I would find him.

As the cruise enthusiast you know me to be, I am always fascinated when I meet someone who makes me look like a rookie. After sharing a cup of coffee one morning with a fine gentleman named Carl, we got to talking about our love for cruise vacations. Carl was getting ready for a 180-day around-the-world cruise by taking the present cruise and two more short cruises before the big event. I asked how many cruises he had taken to date, and he told me sixty-five, which is a few more than I have taken so far. I must have seemed impressed because he told me he was traveling with the woman in his life whom he met on a cruise several years ago when they were traveling as singles. This woman has been on well over three hundred cruises and is the number one sea-day passenger in the history of Princess Cruise Lines. Ilene, it turns out, has been at sea for a number approaching eleven years of her life. If you want to learn more about them and their travels, you will find Ilene Weiner on the internet and in travel magazine articles.

As I told you in the book, you are certain to run into some people almost every day of your cruise. Take Steve the retired liquor store owner, whom I would pass by regularly in the early hours on my way to the fitness center. Steve always had a smile on his face, and I enjoyed the few minutes we got to spend almost every single day talking about family. Steve, like myself, has left his business to his daughter, while I have left mine to my two sons. Similarly, I ran into a lady named Jody on a regular basis. When she learned that I was from Buffalo, all she could do was tell me how much she rooted for the Buffalo Bills.

Because our cruise was one of the very first to sail post-COVID, our ship was sailing at only a fraction of capacity. This fact made it much easier to become acquainted with guests I might otherwise have had an opportunity only to wave at in passing. The same may be said of the opportunity to get to know the ship's officers. The captain was not only visible; he was both personable and informative. At a small group lunch that my wife and I had the pleasure of attending, I met the staff captain, the second-in-command of the ship, and learned much about his family and background in addition to the things I reported about safety and security early on in the book. Sitting next to my wife was the human resources officer, who together with the hotel manager deals with the difficult issues involving staff and crew members. The lunch was not only informative; it proved to be a pleasant way to get to know more about the people wearing the starched shirts and stripes.

When I wrote the chapter about the crew, I told you that if you didn't know a little more than a little about your cabin attendants by the end of the cruise, then you were on the wrong cruise. By the end of this relatively short seven-day journey, my wife and I felt as though we had known Alex and Edy for a very long time. They not only kept our stateroom clean and fresh; they made certain that we had every possible amenity they were able to secure. Ice, fresh orange juice, canapes, and other items were never more than a call and a few minutes away. We also learned about the challenges they endured during the past year and a half. In the end, I got the feeling that they were as happy, if not happier, than we were to be sailing with guests once again.

About the Author

GREG STAMM grew up in the Bronx, New York, as the child of loving, working, middle-class parents. He pitched in as a kid by delivering newspapers, though it was his parents' willingness to dig deep into their pocketbooks that got him sent away from the Bronx for college. There, he quickly became known as the kind of guy who occasionally sought out trouble. He was confronted with a decision to pursue a commission in the United States Army or protest the war in Vietnam. The decision to join up was fortuitous, as the Army sent him to law school instead of Southeast Asia.

After he served for several months under General George Patton in Fort Knox, Kentucky, the end of the Vietnam War meant that Greg could return to civilian life and begin a career in the law. He spent a brief stint in government service before following his independent streak into the decision to open his own practice.

Having lived the life he was born into, he has attempted to walk the walk it has enabled. His father's tragic passing when Greg was only nineteen years old has served as his impetus to live every day as though it might be his last. In that, he knows he has succeeded.

He plans to take many more cruise vacations in the years to come, but his ultimate dream is to sail on an around-the-world cruise. He hopes to see you aboard a cruise vacation in the not-too-distant future.

CPSIA information can be obtained
at www.ICGtesting.com
Printed in the USA
BVHW082022011221
622869BV00007B/165